Love
is like a
Butterfly

BEVERLY PETERSON

authorHOUSE®

AuthorHouse™
1663 Liberty Drive
Bloomington, IN 47403
www.authorhouse.com
Phone: 1-800-839-8640

This is a book of fiction, any name or character resembling persons
living or dead is purely coincidental. All incidents or locations are
products of the author's imagination and are used fictionally.

Published by AuthorHouse 8/1/2013

ISBN: 978-1-4918-0579-4 (sc)
ISBN: 978-1-4918-0578-7 (e)

Library of Congress Control Number: 2013913650

This book is printed on acid-free paper.

Dedication

To my husband who was always there

To encourage me even when I had my

Doubts, and to my daughters and close

Friends that cheered me on.

Chapter 1

Dear Bob:

I am not sure how to explain this to you, but I will try. We have tried talking in the past, but I always felt that you never understood anything that I had said. I need some time for myself, some time to sort through my feelings. Hopefully I can decide what direction my life will take.

No one knows about this letter, and I haven't told anyone where I will be going. The checkbook is in the desk in the kitchen. I have paid all the bills to date, and have made sure that the refrigerator has food in it for now.

I called work and told them I had to take an emergency leave of absence for a few weeks. If anyone asks, just tell them that I have gone to see Joan. Tell them that she called with a family emergency, and since we are best friends, she asked me to come out immediately. I am sure that no one will question you.

Knowing you, I am sure that this will be very embarrassing. I am sorry. I just don't know where to turn or what to do. I have thought about this for a long time, I have to do this, I have no other choice. Please try to understand. If you can't understand, be supportive and give me this time. Don't spend time looking for me. I will call in about two weeks. Hopefully I will be ready to come home within that time. I will be okay, really.

The kids will be home late. They have play practice after school. Donna is giving them a ride home, so you don't have to worry.

I will call you.

Mary

After reading the note over for the fourth time, I am trembling as I fold it and place it in an envelope with Bob's name on it. If I leave it on his dresser he will be sure to see it, and the kids won't find it if by chance they come home before he does.

I can't think about what I am doing any longer. I have to walk out now or I will never do it. One last look around. I have to take one last look.

Candy's room. She certainly is all girl. The curtains and bedspread all pink and ruffly. It doesn't matter that she is grown up at fifteen; she still has stuffed animals lining her room, each with its own special memory. I am sure that she has every one she has ever gotten. As I pick up the pink teddy bear she had as a baby, the music box in it strikes out the final notes of its last wind. I used to put it in her crib when she slept so that she wouldn't feel alone.

Rob the 12th grade heart throb. Someone had tagged that saying to him earlier this year, and it never faded. His room is an example of everything neutral. Nothing personal hanging on his walls to identify him or to give him meaning. He has always been able to hide behind a wall of protection not ever letting anyone see the real Rob. Somewhat like his father. I remember the time he found a bird that was near death in the back yard, and he cared for that bird night and day, nursing it back to health. The day he was finally able to let it go, he stood at the back door for at least an hour watching, and, I suspected, hoping it would return to him, but yet never sharing his feelings with us.

Maybe when I come back, if I come back, I will be able to help him realize that it is all right to be vulnerable to people and family.

I have to leave. Now!

As I place the envelope on Bob's dresser I feel an urgency that tells me to hurry. No one should be home for two hours, yet a warning is making me feel uneasy. I have already packed two suitcases and a garment bag. This should be enough to get me through whatever time I need. I just have to get away.

As I drive out the drive way, one last look. It is a beautiful house, in a setting that anyone would be proud to be a part of it. A brick ranch house with flowers encircling it. We had also planted flowers on each side of the driveway creating a welcome sight to anyone visiting. But material things were never very important to me. Oh sure, I enjoyed everything we were able to buy for ourselves and the kids, but I always seemed to be unhappy. Not so that anyone could see, but down deep in my soul. I guess that I was a little like Rob, usually keeping my doubts and thoughts to myself.

Good-bye Bob. I will call you. I will. Maybe tomorrow.

Chapter 2

I haven't decided where I will stop, but I have decided that I will stay in Wisconsin. It doesn't make too much sense to travel a long distance. I can get lost within a few hours of home. The first nice small town I feel comfortable in will be my home for at least the next few weeks.

It is strange to start driving and not care what highway I am on or what direction I take. Something so completely different from my life at home. Everything is so well planned out without any consideration for me or what I might want to do. My life has rotated around Bob and the kids for so long that I have lost any identity that I had, and have become only a chauffeur and a maid. I have tried to make them understand that I need more in my life, but every time I start this conversation, it is as if no one hears me. Bob keeps reminding me that I expect everything to be perfect, and that life isn't perfect. Is that really what I expect, or do I miss the simple everyday considerations that each of us long for.

Picking up the newspapers off the floor instead of leaving it there for me to pick up, not leaving his glass by his chair side, making the bed when he is the last one out of it. Wouldn't it be nice to come home just once and have a meal started or the dishes put away. No not just once, it would be nice to have that on a regular basis. I work just as much as anyone else, yet when I get home I still have an evening of work to do. I would love to sit down, read the paper, watch television, and have someone else cook the meal and then clean up afterwards. I don't think that this is too much to ask, yet I honestly believe I will never see it. I have tried a number of times to make myself understood, but I always get comments like: "You know I hate to do dishes." As if that is the one thing that I love to do. Or, "If you would plan the meals ahead then I would be glad to help you." I guess I could take time to plan out meals, but how much trouble would it be to come home and find hamburger helper being made in a pan, nothing fancy, or maybe grilled cheese sandwiches. Just the fact someone, just once would say, "Here let me do this for you tonight and you sit".

The kids aren't much better. Oh, they are great if I need help, or if company is coming and I have a mountain of work to do, that is, if I ask them to help. I can never remember either one of them doing a task on their own without being asked to do it. I am sure there were times they did, but right now I can't remember any.

Maybe Bob is right, maybe I do expect everything to go smoothly, perfectly in his words. I don't think I do. What I need is to be loved. I need caring, I need romance. I need Bob to put the paper away for just one evening and notice that I am in the room with him. I need him to hold me after we make love, and not just turn away and say 'good night'. I just need to be held.

The way it looks now, I have to choose between my family and their needs and my own, and I feel outnumbered.

Chapter 3

I realize that I have been driving for almost three hours with a short break at a rest area and one stop for gas. I have always hated driving long distances, but today the time has flown by. It is starting to approach late afternoon, and I better stop at the next town that has a friendly look, and stay the night.

As I enter Midland, I see a small cafe with a number of large trucks in the parking area. Bob had always said that if you are looking for a place to eat, keep an eye open for a restaurant where truckers eat. The food is usually good and the prices reasonable. I made a mental note where it was so that I could come back for supper after I found a place to stay. The town was a small town, with one block of stores on each side of the street. At the end of the downtown area was a gas station, and next to it a grocery store. I stopped at the gas station to ask if there was a motel in town.

"Why lady, you just passed it when you came into town."

"I'm sorry, I must have gone right by it without noticing. Can you tell me where it is?"

"Sure can. Just turn around and go back two blocks. Did you happen to notice a truck stop named Dolly's?"

I nodded that I did.

"Well, the motel is attached to the south side of Dolly's."

I thanked the man, and went back to my car feeling a little sheepish. Here I was in a town that was barely two blocks long in total, and I had missed the only motel. I made my way back to Dolly's Motel, deciding that if I didn't like the look of it I would travel to the next town, even though it was close to dusk.

On closer inspection, Dolly's Motel was a typical eight unit motel. Nothing fancy, no pool, but color TV was advertised on the sign, as if this were something that had been recently added. It did look clean and neat, and I decided that after the emotional strain of leaving home and the driving, I needed to stop and collapse, and Dolly's would be as good as any other.

The office to the motel was in the restaurant. As I approached the cashier, I found out that Dolly really did exist. She was about fifty five years old, medium build, brownish red hair that was pulled back into a French twist, and she was running around the restaurant giving each table her personal touch. When she saw me standing at the cash register, she greeted me with her own special smile that lit up her face.

"Well hi there, can I help you?"

"Is this the office to the motel?"

"Sure is. It just saves me a lot of steps if I have the office in here. Can I help you?"

"I'm interested in renting a room. What is your rate?"

"You look as though you need a rest. Been driving all day? You look all worn out."

When I didn't answer her she continued.

"The rooms are nothing fancy, but I guarantee they are clean. The price is $40.00 a day, and if you stay longer I might be able to give you a good rate."

"That sounds fine. I'll take a room, but only for tonight."

"How many will be staying?"

"Just me."

"Okay honey. Just fill out this form, and I'll get you set up."

"This is really nice" I stated, as I looked around the cafe. There was a counter with about 10 stools, and red checked tablecloths covered the tables that lined the walls. All in the entire cafe could hold about 75 people.

"Thanks. After my divorce I decided that if I was going to make a living I better look out for myself because no one else was going to do it, and I went to the bank and talked them into giving me a loan. Low and behold I opened Dolly's Cafe. Here honey, here's your key. You will be in number 5. You can park your car right in front of the door if you like. After you get settled, if you would like to come back for a cup of coffee and a piece of pie, it's on me."

I thanked her, took the key to room number 5 and went back to my car. As I pulled the car in front of the room, I suddenly felt a loneliness ebbing over me. I had to get my luggage in the room before someone came up to me and asked what was wrong. I have never been good at hiding my feelings and tonight was no exception.

Opening the door I walked into what would be my home for the next few days. The bedspread was a chocolate brown color, with matching curtains. There were pictures on the walls that gave the room a special, personal touch. They were of beautiful landscapes, not the typical motel nonsense pictures. There was also a recliner in the corner with a writing table next to it. The carpeting was of the kitchen carpet variety in brown and beige tweed, not very soft, but very practical. All in all it was very inviting, as inviting as a motel room can be.

As I looked around, it became clear I was alone. There wouldn't be anyone knocking at my door, or anyone calling for my help or advice. I was alone, and that is exactly the way I wanted it. Or did I? Suddenly the loneliness washed over me again, only this time there was no one around, and no reason to hold back the tears. As I collapsed on the bed I sobbed as if my heart was breaking. It was breaking bit by bit, and this time I could cry and not care if anyone heard me. This time I could cry and not stop because I was afraid that someone would see my swollen eyes. Crying was nothing new to me; I seem to be doing a lot of that lately. I could be running an errand, driving down the street, and unexpectedly a wave of emotion would engulf me and suddenly tears would be streaming down my face. No explanation, nothing in particular that I was thinking about, just a deep feeling of being alone. The only thing is, this time I really am alone. There won't be anyone coming home later. This time the answers are up to me. I can no longer push my problems to the back of my mind. I have made the decision to deal with them; there is no turning back, not now.

With that new realization my sobbing turned into a mournful quiet crying. A crying that would not stop, and could only be hushed by welcomed sleep.

Chapter 4

"Good morning. You don't look like you slept too good last night honey." Dolly greeted as she automatically poured a cup of coffee for me. I had hoped I had carefully covered up the puffiness around my eyes to hide the telltale signs of tears from the night before.

"No, I guess I did drive too far yesterday. I didn't realize how exhausted I was. I think I'll just have toast this morning."

"Not much to start the day on honey, but then if you get hungry, you can always stop back for that piece of pie you missed last night."

I had always resented being called "honey" by most people, but coming from Dolly it all seemed natural. I liked her small town welcome and the pleasant look on her face, I could understand why she had the business she did. Everyone liked her and her carefree attitude, yet she also gave the impression that she honestly liked you and was concerned. Like her comment about toast not being much to start off the day. She seemed to really care.

I drank my coffee, and for the first time I noticed my fellow customers. There were four truck drivers sitting at the counter. Around the tables that lined the walls were what I assumed to be locals from the town. Most of the people looked as if they were retired, each of them talking from one table to another. It was clear that Dolly's was the place to come for breakfast, and the morning gossip. When Dolly brought me my toast, I told her that I would be staying a few more days.

"Well glad to have you honey. Are you visiting anyone here, or just escaping?"

My sudden glance must have told her that I was indeed escaping, and surprised that she guessed my secret. I then looked down into my coffee cup away from her eyes. I could feel Dolly's gaze search my face, curious by my sudden quietness and by my feeble attempt to concentrate on the food that lay in front of me.

"I usually don't ask this of strangers, but since you will be staying with me for a few days, you don't by chance need something to keep you busy? I am desperately in need of some help in the restaurant for the next week or two, and if you are interested, you could work off the charge of the room, plus make a few bucks at the same time."

Work. I had never thought about working while I was away. It does make sense. I can't sit in my room all day and all night trying to sort through my feelings. I do need time to; as Dolly put it, escape from my own thoughts.

"It sounds interesting, but I have never waited on tables before."

"Have you ever cleaned up after someone? Or cooked and served diner, and then did the dishes?"

Little did she know that I had done this all my married life? "Yes I have done all those things."

"That is all you have to know. And then, you have to treat the customers as you would like to be treated. That's all. You think about it, and let me know. But if you are interested, you can start this morning about 10:00, or this afternoon around 2:00. It is a little slower at those times, and it will give you time to get used to the routine. I'll check back with you later."

"Dolly, I don't have to think about it. It sounds perfect. It will be just what I need. If you can put up with my mistakes, I promise to work hard for you."

"Great! What was your name again honey?"

"Mary . . . Marilyn."

"Okay Marilyn, come back about 10:00 and I will show you the ropes. Don't worry, everyone here in Midland is friendly to newcomers. It won't be hard to learn." With that she was off to another table, stopping to say a few words as she passed each table.

I did it, I said yes, and I felt good about it. There was no one around to try to change my mind, to try to steer me in another direction. I made my own decision. It wasn't going to be a job of importance, but I was going to pay my own way, and for the first time someone was going to appreciate the work I was doing for them.

Chapter 5

I stood in front of the mirror going over my appearance one last time before I walked over to the restaurant. Even at 38 years old I was still attractive. My short brown hair framed by face with wisps of hair. My dark brown eyes looked dull today. There was no usual laughter in them, no warmth. As I stepped back I could see loneliness staring back at me. I was not going to go to a job and pass along my depression to the customers. If I am going to work for Dolly, I will give her my best effort. I forced a smile. It didn't work. A smile can't be forced. Anyone could see through that in a minute. Again, I smiled, but this time I tried to put some feeling into it. Passable.

I glanced at my watch and saw that it was 9:55. I closed the door behind me and walked toward the restaurant. My stomach was churning with anticipation of my new job, but yet there was a satisfaction that I made this decision. No one had contradicted it; no one had told me how foolish it was. It was a realization that I felt good about not having to justify my actions to anyone. I had never realized how important that feeling was before now.

Dolly was wiping down a table that she had just finished clearing. She was right; it was slow at this time. There were only a few tables occupied, and they were nursing a cup of coffee.

"Hi Hon, you can bring your purse back here, and I will show you the ropes."

I followed Dolly behind the counter, and placed my purse next to hers on a shelf in the kitchen. The kitchen was very small. I was surprised to see everything so compact. Somehow I had felt that the kitchen to a cafe would be larger, but this was only slightly larger than my kitchen at home.

"Lucy, I want you to meet someone. This is Marilyn; she will be waiting on tables for the next few days." I was startled by her use of the name Marilyn, but I will have to get accustomed to it for awhile. "Marilyn, this is Lucy our day cook. This place couldn't run without her great home cooking." Lucy said hi, and I see that she was pleased with the praise coming from Dolly. Lucy is in her mid fifties, graying hair and a little plump. She fit the typical look one imagines when we hear the word grandmother.

"Lucy is a dear. She doesn't talk much, but she is dependable and a great cook. When we get busy, just stay out of her way in the kitchen, she is a whirlwind. Now! You will be responsible for the counter. It is a good place to start. Most of the orders are short, and it will allow you time to get used to where everything is in a hurry. "Dolly then showed me where everything was kept, from the napkins, silverware, cups and saucers, plates, to ketchup bottles, packets of butter and honey. Each had its own organized spot according to the usage. She then gave me a copy of the menu and told me to sit down and read it over.

"You don't have to memorize the prices, write down what the customer asks for, and then while they are eating, you can look up the prices. Just remember to treat them as you would like to be treated. Our motto here is: Service, Service, and Service. Don't worry; I'll be right here if you have a question."

I sat down with the menu in hand. It wasn't too difficult, the typical cafe menu with three specials of the day.

Take an order, give it to Lucy, set the table, get their drinks, pick up the order, give it to the customer, clear the table, and leave the check. This was what I had been doing for years, only I wouldn't have to make the food, or do the dishes.

I looked up as the cafe door opened. I could feel my stomach churning as I anticipated my first customer. I had enough time to read over the menu a number of times, and to get accustomed with the layout of the cafe. I knew where the coffee cups and the water glasses were. That was all I had to worry about now. As I was straightening my apron, I realized that my first customer was already sitting at the counter and patiently waiting for me to gather my courage to wait on him.

"Hi, welcome to Dolly's'. Can I get you a cup of coffee?" I said in the friendliest tone I could muster.

"Coffee would be nice", came the answer.

I grabbed a cup and saucer and carefully poured in the coffee, remembering that I did not appreciate it when a waitress would pour the coffee so fast that it would sometime spill over the edge of the cup. "Remember to treat them as you would like to be treated." Dolly's words came flooding back.

I gave him a menu and told him about the specials for the day, then gave him some time to make up his mind. After straightening the glasses I happened to look up at the customer and saw him sitting there, not looking at the menu, but watching me. I should have been paying closer attention. He must have decided what he wanted, and was waiting to give me his order. I picked up the order pad, took a deep breath, and walked over to him.

"Have you decided what you would like?"

"Could I have some cream for my coffee?"

"Oh, I'm sorry; sure, I'll get some right away." Cream, why hadn't I thought to ask if he needed cream for his coffee? Just because I drink mine black doesn't mean everyone does.

"Is there something else I can get you?"

"I'd like a double cheeseburger. Make sure there is a piece of cheese on each burger, and mayo on the bun."

"That order will be up in just a minute." As I started to walk away he added:

"Could you put onion on that for me, and also make sure that Lucy gives me some French fries with barbecue sauce."

French fries. Why didn't I think to ask if he would like fries? I have to go a little slower and remember to ask.

Lucy, he knew her name. He must be familiar with the cafe, yet didn't say anything when I welcomed him to Dolly's. I gave the order to Lucy, and then walked back to refill his coffee cup.

"You must be a regular here."

"I've been in here before," he said as he quickly made an appraisal of me. "You're new. When did you start?"

"About a half hour ago. Does it show that much?"

"No, it's just that I would remember you if I had seen you before." He didn't take his eyes off my face, as I blushed at his comment. For the first time in a long time I was completely lost for words. He added "My name is Jeff. You will probably be seeing a lot of me. I have a truck route that I run everyday, and I usually stop here for a burger, or a quick cup of coffee depending on how much time I have." He took another sip of coffee, and smiled ever so slightly, making me very uncomfortable. I tried to tell myself I should be flattered, it has been a long time since anyone had looked at me that way, but I had also been around long enough to realize when someone was using body language to make an impression on me. He certainly knew how to use every part of his body. Jeff looked as though he was 35, tall, about 6'2", with blonde hair that was slightly wavy. He had dark brown eyes, and a golden tan that accentuated his eyes and hair. His smile was immediate and friendly, almost boyish, yet he had a down south charm about him that could pull even the most guarded individual into his powers.

I brought him his burger, ketchup, mustard, barbecue sauce for his fries, and salt and pepper. I was sure I had remembered everything this time.

"Is there anything else I can get you?"

"Yes, as a matter of fact there is. You never told me your name, or where you are from."

"My name? Well, my name is Mar—Marilyn. I'm from out of state. I just happened to stop by the motel and Dolly said that she needed help. I may be staying for a week or so, and then I should be on my way."

I suddenly stopped talking. Now why did I tell this stranger that I was staying at the motel and would be here for a week or so? I have to be careful not to talk too much.

"Well Marilyn, it's a pleasure to meet you. I hope maybe you will decide to spend more than a week here. You are a real improvement to the scenery." With that, he winked at me and slowly took another sip of his coffee, still watching every move I made from behind his cup. I smiled at the comment and picked up the rag that is used to wipe down the counter and tried to look busy as I re-wiped the already clean counter. I was thankful when another customer came in the door and sat just a few seats away from Jeff. For some reason he made me feel uncomfortable.

"Hi Jeff. Looks like you're a little ahead of your run today."

"Yeah, I even have time to have lunch today", Jeff replied, and went back to concentrating on his burger.

As I approached the next customer, I could feel Jeff's eyes watching me. I looked up at him for just a minute and he immediately smiled.

"Just coffee", the new customer said, and continued talking to Jeff as if I wasn't there. He had a dark blue suit on with a coordinating tie, and if I had to guess by his appearance, I would say that he was a banker or a lawyer. I filled his cup and remembered to give him cream and sugar before I found other busy work to do so I would not intrude on their conversation. This new customer reminded me of Bob. He was attractive, well dressed, and knew exactly what he wanted, and wasn't afraid to ask for it.

I would often fill Bob's coffee cup and he wouldn't even notice I was there. He would be busy reading the paper, and never look up once to say thank you. I was sure this man was the same way.

"Miss, can I have more coffee?"

In an instant, I was transported from my own kitchen back to the diner. I filled his cup and checked with Jeff to see if everything was okay. The man emptied his coffee cup, dropped two quarters on the counter and left as quickly as he came, no acknowledgment that I was even there. I wasn't surprised, I knew his type. He thought he was a little better than anyone else, and I should be happy to wait on him.

"He's not such a bad egg," Jeff said. "You just have to get used to him and his ways."

"What?"

"You are looking at him as if you know him, and don't really approve of him or his attitude. Does he remind you of someone?"

"I think everyone knows someone like him. He's important, he's in charge, and he wants everyone to know it."

"You're right, but there is another side of him that you don't see. His wife has been sick for many years and he has taken care of her himself. Others might have put her in a home, or hired someone to take care of her, but not Chuck. He spends every spare minute he has with her, doing simple things like brushing her hair, things that say 'I love you' without saying it. Don't be too quick to judge him. Everyone has feelings they don't show to people, and Chuck shows them though his actions, not his words."

I felt a little guilty about my quick judgment of Chuck. I was sorry to hear about his wife and surprised to hear about his caring attitude towards her. I never would have guessed that about him, considering how he acted when he strolled into the cafe, the way he barked his order for coffee. No, I certainly would not have guessed that there was another side to him.

"Marilyn! Where were you just now?"

"Oh! My mind must have wondered."

"You know the look you were giving Chuck as he left was a strange look, not really angry or mean, but like he hurt your feelings."

"He just reminds me of someone I know."

"Someone special?"

"No, just someone." I answered as I filled Jeff's coffee cup, picked up the rag, and wiped the already clean counter once again.

Chapter 6

"Mary! Hey Mary! Where are you? I need you to fix me a sandwich as soon as you can. I have another meeting at the office tonight."

Bob rifled through the mail that was lying on the counter.

Mary better make sure we have enough money in the check book before she sends these bills off, Bob thought. Mary has always taken care of these matters, she just does it better than me.

"Mary! Mary! Where are you?"

Bob walked towards the bedroom already removing his dark blue suit coat and loosening his tie. A sweater would be appropriate for the meeting, and a lot more comfortable that his suit. As Bob entered the bedroom, he noticed an envelope on his dresser marked simply—Bob.

"Dear Bob

I am not sure how to explain this to you—" "What the hell is this?" He exclaimed as he scanned the letter.

"Mary where are you?" he bellowed as he ran into the other rooms of the house, also checking the basement. She was nowhere to be found. Bob quickly ran back to the bedroom and sat on the bed. He took the note in his hand and slowly, slowly reread it.

"Direction my life will take . . . embarrassing . . . understand . . . be supportive? What the hell is going on?

Where is she?"

Bob just sat there on the bed not knowing what had happened to the happy life he had when he had left for work that morning. His head was spinning. Had Mary been planning this for a long time? Obviously she had. You don't just leave one day without giving it a lot of thought. Her clothes. Did she take her clothes?

Bob opened the closet doors and checked her side of the closet. There were a few empty hangers, but if he had to, he couldn't tell what she had in there. He just never noticed. He went to her dresser and opened the drawers. And then the realization finally hit him. Her underwear was gone. The empty hangers must have been from things she had taken with her. The letter wasn't a joke, it wasn't a hoax, and she was gone.

Bob was getting angry. What did she have to be unhappy about? She had a nice house didn't she? She had nice clothes didn't she? He let her work because she said that she needed something in her life to make her feel worthwhile. He wasn't happy about it, but he did let her work. What was going on? Bob couldn't seem to get past his anger. Mary had some nerve just leaving without giving him a clue what was wrong. What did she expect him to do? After all the kids would be coming home and what did she expect him to tell them? Bob went back and reread the note again. He couldn't believe she had gone.

Chapter 7

"Marilyn, you have been doing great for your first day."

"Thanks Dolly, I appreciate the kind words." As we were putting the chairs up on the tables, getting ready for the night cleaners, I had a sense of accomplishment. I had enjoyed my first day working at the cafe. I had never really had the time to observe other people. My life had always been so full of my own schedules and those of my family, I had been missing the world going on around me. It was interesting, now thinking back on some of the people that came into the cafe.

There was that young couple that came in this afternoon, so much in love with each other they hardly even noticed everyone else. It was nice to see him open the door for her, and wait until she sat down before he did. You don't often see such manners now days. All through their meal they didn't stop holding hands on top of the table, and the gazes towards each other told me that they weren't aware of the world around them.

The family of four was such a contradiction from the couple. The husband and wife seem to be in their middle thirties, along with their two small children, both boys, about eight and ten years old. They sat down in a booth near the windows, and for the first ten or fifteen minutes they didn't have much to say to each other. As the boys became restless they started teasing each other. The father became mad and loudly reprimanded them while the cafe looked on. The mother seemed embarrassed, and the boys sat very still not looking to the right or to the left. Throughout the evening I could see the mother running referee between the boys, so not to get their father upset. What was to be a special night out became a night of strained emotions for everyone.

The lonely man sitting in the corner facing the entire cafe, so he could see everyone as they came in and left. I had discovered that he was a widower, and came in each day. I guessed that he had been very dependent upon his wife, and was lonelier than anything else. He seemed to know everyone, one of the benefits of a small town, but yet no one asked him to join their table of family or friends. Everyone stopped to say "hi" or just a few words, yet no one included him. Very sad to see, if only someone would take the time to notice.

"Say Honey, are you pooped, or would you like to join me over at The Office for a beer?"

"The Office?"

"Yea, it's just a neighborhood bar. I usually go next door for a beer to unwind before I go home. By the end of the day it is nice to have someone wait on me for a change."

"It sounds very nice right about now."

As we walked through the parking lot of the two neighboring businesses I could see The Office ahead. It was a small square building sided in a natural wood. The windows showed beer lights calling to all who passed by. As we walked in, the interior was almost as dark as it was getting outside. A few wall lights added just enough light along with the beer signs to allow you to see where you were going. Dolly leads me to a table close to the wall and it was great just to sit and relax.

"Hi Dolly. Done for another day?" The waitress asked as she was eyeing me. "What can I get your friend here?"

"What are you going to have Dolly?"

"Beer. I always have a tap beer. A creature of habit I guess."

"I'll have the same." I had never liked beer, but feeling a little out of place, I desperately wanted to fit in.

"This is Marilyn; she is staying with me for a few days and has been good enough to help me out. She's doing one heck of a good job for being her first day."

I now felt the same pride I saw in Lucy, the cook, when Dolly complemented her work. Dolly may be a small town businesswoman, but she knew the right words to say about her employees.

"Now Hon, why don't you tell me something about yourself."

I was not prepared for her question, and felt nervous about answering it.

"Nothing much to tell, I was just driving through and decided to stop for the night. When you asked me if I would be interested in working I said, Why not? I'm not on a time schedule so my time is my own."

As the waitress sat the beers in front of us, I could see that Dolly was studying my face. I picked up the beer and took a sip. I still don't like the taste of beer, but it did taste better than I remembered it. It must have something to do with working so hard, and finally being able to sit and relax.

"I know it is none of my business Hon, but if the time ever comes when you want to talk, I'm here. I'm not a professional councilor or anything like that, but I have a good ear, a good shoulder to cry on, and I never gossip about anyone, you included."

I didn't say anything for a few minutes. How had she guessed I was hiding something? It would be nice to have someone to talk to. She doesn't know me or my family. It wouldn't be as though I would be talking to someone that was a friend to Bob, or to the children. I do think I could trust her.

"What, do you think I am in some sort of trouble?"

"I'm not sure. I only know you are hiding something, maybe running away from something, and I also know that there is a great deal of sadness hiding behind your eyes. You try to hide it, but it's there just the same."

Tears started streaming down my face. Everything I had bottled up inside came rushing out. Not in a fitful sobbing, but in a gentle stream of hurt, welling up and over my eyelashes.

"You're right I am running away. I just need some time to figure out what I am going to do."

"You got a husband somewhere? And some kids?"

"How did you know?"

"Your ring finger on your left hand. You took off your wedding rings, but the impression was left on your finger. I also noticed your bumper sticker on your car. You are a member of the sports booster club at a high school. I just figured you were a parent or supported the local high school."

"Do you always notice things like that about people?"

"Once you get used to working here, you will notice a lot about people. You can put pieces of information together like a puzzle, and then just wait and watch to see if your intuition was right. After all these years I am usually right."

Dolly took a sip of her beer, and then, just sat there waiting. She wasn't going to push me into something I wasn't ready for, on the other hand she would be a good listener if I wanted her to be.

The tears swelled up again in my eyes. I desperately wanted to talk to someone, but I had always been such a private person. I always prided myself on being able to handle my own problems, and I was the one that always provided the shoulder for others to cry on. Why is it this time I felt so abandoned, so alone.

"Dolly, I would like to talk to you, I just don't know if you could understand."

"Hon, I see a lot of people come and go at the cafe and motel. I won't pretend to understand all of them. If I could write a book they wouldn't believe everything I have seen. Something's are spicier than the soap operas would ever dream of, and other things are so dull, no one would be interested. If you need to talk, I'll be glad to listen. I don't have anything to do for the next couple of hours, and who knows, maybe we'll solve the world's problems in that time."

"Dolly, I have left my husband and two children." In just verbalizing it I felt as though a load was lifted from my shoulders. "Yesterday I wrote a note that I was leaving, packed my bags, and just left. What's worse is I don't feel guilty, I feel sad, but not guilty."

Dolly didn't say anything, she just sat there, not surprised, not shocked, and just listening.

"I have been unhappy for a number of years. I have tried to talk to my husband about it, but he never understands. He thinks everything is fine, and he just has to humor me for awhile when I am in one of 'my moods'. I'm really at the end of my ropes; I didn't know what to do or who to turn to. Bob, that's my husband, won't go for counseling, because he doesn't think there is anything wrong. He is happy, and he doesn't understand why I'm not. I love my kids, but I had to get away for my own sanity."

When I started talking, everything came flooding out. I could not have stopped the words if I had wanted to. I had been holding back so much emotion for so long it was like a swollen river spilling over its banks, nothing could stop the flow.

Dolly reached over and covered my hands with her own. I could see sympathy, no, understanding in her eyes.

"What did you tell your family in your note?"

"I said that I needed time to sort through my feelings. I told Bob that I would call him in about two weeks. I had paid all the bills, put food in refrigerator, called work to tell them I had to go to a friend that needed me and I would be gone for a couple of weeks. I also made arrangements for a friend to pick up the kids. I know Bob will be angry, he never seems to understand me, but I had to do it Dolly, I just had to. I don't how much longer I could have stayed and kept my sanity."

"Hon, do you know what I just heard?"

I lifted my tear stained face to her and slowly shook my head no, almost afraid of her response.

"I heard a very unhappy wife and mother, who took the time to take care of her family, when she was feeling desperate herself. Marilyn, you paid bills, you filled the refrigerator, you called into your work, made arrangements for your children, and then you took time for yourself. Even in running away, you put your family ahead of yourself. You placed yourself in second position. I have a feeling you've done that for along time."

Tears rolled down my cheeks with a relief I had not found before this. Finally, finally someone understood me. She didn't see me as a bad person, and she wasn't closing off her feelings to me.

"You mean you aren't ashamed of how I acted towards my husband and my children?"

"Ashamed? How could I be ashamed? You must have felt desperate to take the measures you did in order to sort through your feelings."

"Yes, yes that's it exactly!"

"I wish I could help you Marilyn, but I'm afraid this is something you will have to find answers to yourself."

"Dolly, you have helped me already in just listening to me and not judging me."

Chapter 8

The kids should be home any minute now, what am I going to tell them? A wife doesn't just leave her husband and children to 'find herself'. I wonder what is really going on. Did she leave to meet a man somewhere? Where is she? How does she expect to manage without me? How is she going to find somewhere to stay? Or does she already have a place to stay, and who is she with?

Bob crumpled the note with his fist and threw it into the wastebasket.

"Damn her, damn her! She has some nerve! Couldn't she have given me some warning that she was leaving? You don't all of a sudden wake up one morning and say 'I think I'll run away today'. Who is she with?"

"Hi Dad. You should see how the play is coming. I hope you know your daughter is the star of the whole production." Candy bubbled as she threw her coat on the couch. She fell exhausted in the matching beige chair, and kicked off her shoes into the middle of the room. Rob had dropped his books on the counter next to his sisters, but had then taken his coat into his room, and changed into a T-shirt and sweat pants. When he came back into the living room Candy was still exploding with enthusiasm about the play.

"Candy, I know this is the first play you have been in, but it really isn't that big of a deal," Rob said.

"Just because you hang around in the back room working on props doesn't mean that you are an expert on plays, and how exciting they are."

"You wouldn't be in anything exciting if it weren't for the props and the scenery. And what makes you such an expert? You aren't one of the main characters."

"I'm also an understudy. You know what happens if Mary Sue is sick or if she can't finish it? I'll take over that's what it means."

"Kids, stop that bickering. I don't need this tonight. Candy, pick up your coat and put your shoes away. Rob, go in and start your homework"

"Where's Mom? When's supper going to be ready?" Candy asked as she quickly changed the subject knowing that her father was not in any mood to deal with her and Rob tonight. Little did she realize that her question would not be a welcome change in subjects?

"Dad, where is Mom? Is she working late tonight? Dad . . . what's going on? Where's Mom?"

Bob had not had enough time to think how he was going to handle this with the kids. He didn't want to worry them, but yet they were old enough to realize the ramifications of their mothers' acts. He owed it to them to be honest. They should know just what she had done.

"Your Mom . . . . got a call from Joan today. She has a family emergency and asked if your mother could come out to see her immediately. She'll be gone for about two weeks, so that means we all have to chip in together so everything runs smooth. That means everyone does their share of work, and I mean everyone!" Bob just couldn't tell them the truth, not yet anyway. And who knows, maybe she will be back in just a day or two. She will be back and begging my forgiveness, wishing that she had never left in the first place.

"Joan's! That was sudden. When did she call? Mom didn't say anything about this before I left for school." Rob . . . always the logical one. Bob would have to be careful not to let him see how concerned he already was.

"Your right, it was all of a sudden, but I really think we can manage for a week or two don't you? Now, get started on your homework while I see what is in the refrigerator for supper."

Rob seemed to accept everything for now, and turned to go back to his room. He turned to look back at Bob with a questioning look on his face before turning the corner, but Bob was already in the refrigerator scrutinizing its contents with a frown on his face.

"Dad fix dinner, that a new one."

Chapter 9

I heard the buzzing, but it took a few minutes to get myself acclimated to my new home. I turned off the alarm and fell back into bed. I felt drained and very tired. I am normally a morning person, able to get out of bed with little or no effort regardless of the night before, but this morning I didn't even want to think about getting out of bed, I only wanted to close my eyes and slowly let myself ebb away into deep sleep.

"Oh my! I have to go to the cafe this morning."

I jumped out of bed and made my way to the shower. Why do I feel so groggy? I turned on the light in the bathroom and what looked back at me in the mirror gave me a start. I saw a face with no life. My eyes were swollen with bags under them from the emotions that spilled over last night. I would really have a major job of concealing with my make-up before I went to work.

I wonder how Bob and the kids are doing today. Did Bob get up in time to get the kids off to school? Oh no, I forgot to tell him to be sure and give the kids enough money for lunch tickets.

Suddenly the tears started again. Perhaps I shouldn't have left. I don't know of anyone who is happy, all the time, but I haven't felt really happy in years. No! I won't do this to myself again. I have a right and a duty to myself to decide if this is the future I want. I know it won't change unless I am willing to make the sacrifice to change it. I shook my head as if trying to throw all the negative thoughts out of my mind, took a deep breath, and smiled at myself in the mirror. I will be OK I turned to turn the shower on, and as I reached back to get a towel, I saw the same sad face looking back at me in the mirror, but this time I saw a plea of "Don't give up on me, we can make a difference".

Before opening the door to the cafe, I stood up straight, threw my shoulders back, put a smile on my face, and took a deep breath. Now, I'm ready for another day.

"Hi Dolly."

"Hi Hon; looks like it is going to be a busy day today. Sure glad you decided to stay a few days, you're a great help to me."

As I put my purse in the back room and grabbed an apron I tried to decide if Dolly's comments were said to help my mood for the day, or if she really meant it. At this point I don't care, all I know is, her simple words made me feel better already.

As I walked out into the cafe and assessed the customers, Dolly was right, we were busy. I immediately grabbed a tub and started to bus the tables. As I emptied each table of dirty dishes and wiped it clean, I took a few seconds to reset it, getting it ready for the next customer. Within fifteen minutes I had cleared the tables and had taken the dishes back into the kitchen. I grabbed the coffee pot and made the rounds to each table filling the already empty coffee cups, remembering to take some packets of coffee creamer in my apron so I was prepared and didn't have to make another trip back to the kitchen. Within an hour most of the customers had finished their breakfast and were on their way to work, or back home.

As the last table of six walked out the door, I could feel my tension leave. Now I could work a little slower for a few hours before the lunch crowd came in. I was really enjoying this job, almost more than any other I had before.

Job. I wonder how they were coming at the insurance office. Ours was one of the few remaining offices that would file insurance claims for our clients. We had a number of senior citizens that were so thankful for our help. Some of them had never done any kind of bookwork, and suddenly found themselves alone with no one to turn to. It is so difficult to learn new habits when one loses a partner. I not only filed claims, I helped some of them balance checkbooks, show them how to write checks, pay bills, and even encourage them to get out and join groups so they could make new friends. I have always felt more comfortable with people older than myself, therefore I never minded when someone asked for help. They were always so appreciative, and sincere. I did miss my clients. They have not only been my work, but also my lifeline these past years. In going to work, I was able to blot out my feelings and escape for eight hours each day. Not a long time, but long enough to hold myself together.

Ours was only a three person office, the agent, me, and a part-time office girl. It will be difficult for them to carry on without me. Sharon, our part-time girl, knows everything I do, but it is second nature to me, and she will have a hard time getting everything done on time.

Jim, my boss, was really good when I called and told him I would like to have an emergency leave. I started to explain about Joan, and he stopped me saying I didn't have to explain. He knew me well enough to know I wouldn't ask for an emergency leave unless that's exactly what it was.

"Marilyn, why don't you take a break and have a cup of coffee? I bet you haven't even had time for one yet."

Dolly was right. We have been so busy since I walked in the door; I haven't even been able to wake up with my usual cup of coffee.

"Would you like me to pour you a cup too?"

"Sure, I guess I could use a break too."

Dolly grabbed the cup of coffee I poured, and slid into one of the seats at the counter with a sigh of relief.

"It sure seems good to sit for a minute."

"Yes it does."

There was a strained silence between us. I wasn't sure what to say to Dolly. I appreciated her support last night, but deep down I still wasn't sure how she felt about me.

"Dolly, you have been great to me. I want you to know I value your friendship. No one has ever understood me like you do. I needed it, especially last night."

"Hon let me ask you something, have you ever told anyone how you feel? Have you ever told them your feeling, the ones that come from deep down?" She touched her midriff to emphasize her words.

I never have. I had a few close friends, but they were all so happy in their marriages I didn't think that anyone would understand something I couldn't explain myself.

"No, not completely."

"You know that saying, "In order to have a friend you have to be one?" Well there is another side of that too. If you want to have a friend, you have to be able to confide in her, you have to trust her. Not that she necessarily understands every situation, but you have to trust her that she won't judge you, but she will listen and be there for you. All I did was listen to you. I listened to your words, not your grief. In listening to your words, I saw a caring mother and wife that had put her life on hold, and you seem to need permission from someone to say it is all right to want something more. I don't want you to be too hard on yourself. Everything you have been doing all these years has been a choice you made. You love your children; I know you aren't sorry you had them."

"Oh no, I wanted them. I planned them."

"And your husband, I'm sure you loved him at one time, and I have the feeling you still love him."

"I'm not sure how I feel. I know I can't keep going on the way I have been."

"Marilyn, when your children were born, they needed you full time. When they were toddlers, they depended upon you for everything, food, clean clothes, hugs and kisses, but they are almost adults. You don't have to continue to mother them unless that is your choice."

"I can't just abandon them!" As soon as I said those words, I realized how foolish it sounded. That is exactly what I had chosen to do.

"You are still a very important member of your family, and I am sure they still depend on you for support, but what I am saying is that they are old enough to take on Responsibilities of their own, you don't have to do everything."

I knew she was right. I think I found it easier to do things myself than to continually harp at the kids to do their share.

"I am going to say one more thing, and then I will get off my soapbox. Your husband, Bob I think you said? You have to look at your whole life. If you can say that you aren't happy, and you think you would be better off without him, then make your decision and begin a life without him. Don't be like a yo-yo going from one decision to another, and then back again. It is too hard on you emotionally. But let me give you a warning. Be sure of your answer. A lot of guys may look great out there, but there aren't many worth even giving a second look to."

I looked at Dolly with questions in my eyes.

"Yes, I'm talking from experience. I haven't met one guy worth giving up a night in front of TV or a good book for. I'm not sorry I got my divorce, but divorce isn't for everyone, in fact at times it can be downright hard. Take a look around here, this can be one of the best schools of human behavior there is. Look beyond the people that ask for a hamburger."

Just then Jeff came walking through the door.

"All right you two, get busy or I'll tell the boss."

"It's OK honey, I have an in with the boss."

Dolly got up and picked up her cup and went into the kitchen leaving me to cover the counter.

"Hi Jeff, what can I get you?"

"Just a cup of coffee. I have a long run today, so I won't be back until about eight this evening. That's why I thought I would stop in now."

"Coffee with cream right?" remembering from yesterday.

"Right. Marilyn, I didn't mean I stopped for coffee because I wouldn't be here later, I meant I had a reason for stopping."

"Oh?"

I must have looked surprised because he looked at me for quite awhile and then he realized my surprise was genuine.

"You don't know do you? You really don't know you are the reason I stopped by?"

"Me?"

"I haven't met anyone as unaffected as you in a long time. Most women have their emotions so well hidden I never know what they really think. Marilyn, when I come back in town, how about you and I go out for a drink?"

"Oh Jeff, I don't know."

"It's only for a drink. Ask Dolly, she will tell you I'm harmless. Think about it, I'll stop by your room and you can tell me then. Don't get nervous, nothing serious, just friends having a drink. Think about it."

With that he finished his coffee, and was out the door.

A drink, with Jeff, I don't know. I haven't been out with anyone that wasn't my husband since we were married nineteen years ago. It would be nice to have someone just to talk to. I have always preferred the company of men to women, I'm not sure why, but that is the way it has always been. Bob was always so threatened by my male friends, I was never allowed to have any good male friends, but Bob isn't here now, this is my decision.

"Dolly, let me ask you something. What do you think of Jeff?"

I could see her eyebrow lift just a little.

"Jeff? He's a nice enough guy. Why do you ask?"

"He asked me to go out for a drink tonight."

"What did you say?"

"I didn't say anything; he said he would stop back at eight if I wanted to go."

"What are you going to do?"

"I don't know."

"Nervous?"

I looked at Dolly without answering. I was sure she knew I was.

"Marilyn, it's a drink. That's all a drink. Nothing more. Who knows, this may be just what you need to observe others at the bar. A chance to see what I have been telling you. There isn't much out there."

Almost eight o'clock. I still don't know if I should go out with Jeff or not. Should? I mean I don't know if I want to go out with Jeff. He has been so nice and polite to me at the cafe. I remember him talking about Chuck, trying to explain why he acted so abrupt, almost rude. Jeff was very kind in giving him the benefit of the doubt, understanding that he did not have an easy life.

Brushing the last hair in place I gave myself one more look in the mirror. I guess all along I knew I would go out with Jeff tonight. I chose just the right sweater and jeans, something comfortable but careful not to be suggestive. I chose the hot pink angora sweater. The cowl collar was flattering to me, framing my face with soft lines, while complementing my dark color. A simple gold chain, loop earrings and I was ready. As I stepped back for a final check I frowned at the jeans I was wearing. It was acceptable here in Midland for anytime of day, but being used to dress slacks and not the casual look, I felt somewhat uncomfortable.

The knock on the door startled me. As I opened the door I blushed slightly at the smile that grew on Jeff's face as he saw me standing there.

"Wow, if I knew you were going to be this beautiful, I wouldn't have waited until eight o'clock!"

"Thank you," I said as I quickly turned to get my purse and jacket hiding the blush I felt rising in my face.

"No, thank you." Jeff stood there looking at me. Then as if someone had snapped their fingers to get his attention, he took my jacket in his hands, and gently laid it over my shoulders. His hands on my shoulders gave me a strange tingle that I haven't felt in years. With a quick squeeze he added, "I'm glad you said yes tonight, I've been thinking about you all day."

Chapter 10

"Dad I need money for lunch", Candy yelled.

"Me too!" Rob added.

"Lunch money! How much do you need?"

"Ten dollars", they each yelled from their own rooms as they were finishing getting ready for school.

"Ten dollars! How often do you have to have lunch money?"

"Each week Dad. You eat lunch don't you? Well, so do we."

I could hear the antagonism coming from Rob's voice.

"Look, all I did was ask how much you needed and how often you have to have this much."

"I know Dad, but anytime we need anything, and we have to ask you for it, we have to go through the third degree".

"That's not true. Don't you think I deserve to know where twenty dollars of my money will be going, and how often you need it? What am I expected to do, just hand over money whenever you ask for it?"

"Dad, it's not a big deal," Candy interrupted. "Mom always left the money on our dressers; we never even had to ask for it. I guess we just aren't used to having to ask." Candy, always the peace maker, just like her mother.

Her mother; if Mary hadn't left I wouldn't even have to be bothered with all this. I hope she understands the mess she caused by running away. I have more important things to worry about then trying to remember lunch money.

"Dad, the phone is for you."

"Hello."

"Hi Bob, this is Sally. Say, I know it's my turn to pick the kids up after play practice, but do you think you can do this for me? I wouldn't ask, but Dale's mother is being transferred to the nursing home today, and I just feel as though I should be able to be there for her, it will be traumatic enough without me having to leave early to pick them up."

Pick up the kids? That means running all over the other side of town delivering Tom and Jessie. What do I say? I don't have any choice.

"Sally, don't worry about it, I'll pick up the kids."

"Thanks Bob. I appreciate it. To tell you the truth, I was a little nervous asking you, I knew Mary wouldn't have minded, but I wasn't sure how you would feel."

"You didn't think I would understand?"

"Oh sure, but I know how Andy hates to drive all over the city delivering the kids, so I guess I thought you would feel the same. It's nice to know that there is at least one husband that understands someone has to be responsible for the kids and that someone isn't just the mother. Thanks again Bob, I'll remember to tell Mary how lucky she is."

"Bye Sally, talk to you later."

What did she say? 'Someone has to be responsible for the kids and that someone isn't just the mother.' Is that what

Mary has been trying to get across to me? Well, I don't care she should have just talked to me. I would have understood. I don't know if I can or will forgive her for this stunt she pulled. No one just runs away and deserts their family. Sure, I let her take most of the responsibility of raising the kids, but she is much better at talking to them than I am. It's just easier for her.

"Dad, can you take me to the mall tonight? I just have to get a new outfit for the dance this Friday."

"New outfit? You must have dozens of outfits you have never worn hanging in your closet. Wear one of them."

"Daddy! Ben asked me to go to the dance. I have to have something new to wear. Please!"

"We'll talk about it after school Candy."

"Why can't you ever understand? Just once I wish you would say 'Sure honey, I'll be glad to', just once I would like to hear that."

"Candy, I said we would talk about it after school and I meant it. I have too much on my mind to talk about it now."

"Mom would understand."

"Mom isn't here, I am. If you keep up this attitude we won't even discuss it tonight. Now you can act like an adult and discuss it later, or you can forget it altogether."

Candy stood there and stared at me, then turned on her heel and stormed off to her room without another word.

Kids. Why can't they understand? I can't deal with much more.

Chapter 11

Jeff and I walked down to The Office bar. It was a beautiful night. The stars were bright as diamonds and the moon was shining through streaks of clouds that covered it like angel hair.

"Isn't it beautiful out tonight?" Jeff said.

"Yes, it is."

"You say that with a strange sound in your voice."

"I'm not use to men noticing things like the beauty of the night."

"You aren't? Then the men you are used to being around are missing a lot if they don't notice what's around them."

I couldn't reply to his comment, sensitivity is something I was not used to.

Jeff opened the door for me, and as we walked in the bar he placed his hand at the small of my back to direct me towards a booth. Just the touch of his hand gave me a feeling that I was important to Jeff. Nothing special, just a closeness I had not felt for a long time.

He was known by everyone in the bar, and apparently well liked.

As we sat down, the same waitress that waited on Dolly and me the night before came over to our table. I could tell she recognized me from the other night. Her attention did not stay with me however; instead her eyes were devoted to Jeff.

"Well hi there handsome. I've missed you around here."

"Hi Sheila. I've been busy, gone a lot. Have you met Marilyn?"

"Yes I have. Have you been out of town?"

Interesting. She didn't blink an eye or even acknowledge me with a nod. All responses were left for Jeff. There must be a history there.

"Well, let's just say I have been making a lot of runs."

"What would you like to drink Marilyn?"

"Beer is fine."

"I'll have a brandy seven and a beer for Marilyn."

"If you don't mind, a brandy and seven sounds great."

"Ok, two brandy and sevens."

The waitress gave Jeff a special smile, and turned and walked away, not giving me a second glance.

"You don't have to drink the same thing I am, if you would prefer a beer its fine with me."

"No really, I would rather have a brandy and seven. When I came here with Dolly the other evening, she was drinking beer, and I did order the same thing then, just to fit in, but I have never acquired a taste for beer."

"Just to fit in?"

"Dolly asked me here after work and I . . . it seemed important at the time."

"Here's your drinks Jeff, now don't be a stranger." As the waitress set her drinks down, she gave Jeff that special smile again before she turned and walked away.

"A friend?" I asked.

"A friend. She has made it clear that she would like to be more than a friend, but I have also seen her with other men, and she isn't what I am looking for."

"And what are you looking for?"

"Are you asking out of curiosity or for information for yourself?"

I blushed and looked down at my drink realizing how forward my comment must have sounded.

"Jeff, I didn't mean . . . I was just making conversation."

"You know that is the second time you have done that."

"What"

"Blushed. That's something I haven't seen in quite a while. Don't change, I like it."

There was an awkward silence when Jeff finally answered my original question.

"Sheila has been in Midland for about ten years. She's a single parent, and basically a very nice person. I'm not sure if I can define what I am looking for, but Sheila isn't it. She is nice to have a drink with, or go out to dinner with, but nothing serious, nothing long term. I'm looking for someone that will be as committed to me as I will be to her. I want someone I can laugh with, someone I can love and know she loves me too, but I also want someone who will be there for me in the bad times as well as the good. If I'm ever able to find someone like that, I will never take her for granted. I will love her, and tell her I love her every day. I've seen too many people loose what is most precious to them because they became too busy or too distracted to see what was happening to their lives . . . I will not settle for anything less. I may be alone for a long time, but love is too precious, too special, to settle for anything else."

As he finished talking about his feelings, his mind was far away and his dark eyes were fixed on his hands caressing his drink. His hands were large, dwarfing the glass. The muscles in his arms were twitching as if responding to a memory his mind was now reliving."

"Were you talking about yourself just now? About being too busy to see what was happening to your life?"

Jeff looked up at me surprised by my question. He smiled slightly and the expression on his face softened.

"Tell me a little bit about yourself." Jeff replied.

"Me, there isn't much to tell. I work for an insurance office, I had some vacation time coming, and so I decided to see the countryside . . . wha la . . . I'm here."

"And that's all?"

"What more could there be?"

Suddenly my eyes were drawn to a couple sitting at a table not far from us. They seemed to be so much in love, holding their hands under the table trying to be inconspicuous. They were lost in each other's words, and the sight of their happiness brought tears to my eyes.

"Marilyn, what is it? I have watched you since the first day we met. I have seen the pain in your eyes when a parent reprimands a child too harshly, I see the compassion when someone sits alone, and I see the hurt when you are watching a couple sitting together, not saying anything as if they were with a stranger. Now I can see tears in your eyes that you are trying to hide. What causes this passion in your?"

"Passion?"

"When I use the word passion, I'm talking about the intensity of emotions you feel. You don't feel anything on the surface. Your feelings run very deep. You see more than most people when you are observing."

I couldn't believe the words I was hearing. I have only known Jeff a few days and he seems to understand me. I feel so at home with him, so comfortable. I wonder what he would say if he knew the turmoil I left behind me. He obviously is critical of people or he wouldn't be able to define the person he is looking for like he did. I wonder if he could understand me if he knew my real situation.

"I'm beginning to realize what the important things in life are. Like you, I understand how fragile relationships are and how much you have to work on them. Jeff you never answered my question before, were you talking about yourself?"

Again Jeff looked down at his drink as if trying to find an answer in the ice floating in front of him. He looked up and searched my eyes for a moment and finally added;

"Marilyn, I don't often talk about myself. I'm not sure if it's because men don't discuss their inner feelings. I have never felt comfortable; no safe is the word, talking about my feelings to anyone."

"Don't you mean you have never trusted anyone enough to open up your feelings to them?"

"Maybe you're right. I became vulnerable when someone else knows me from the inside out. Something tells me you would understand. I have an impression that you have a lot you could talk about if you only let yourself."

I felt my throat close with emotion. I tried to regain my composure. My eyes worked against me as I fought hard to hold back the tears, and they spilled over my lashes and slid down my cheek.

Jeff reached over the table and gently touched my face wiping away each tear.

"Here, take my hand." He reached toward me with his palm facing upward. I placed my hand in his as he pulled me up from my seat and led me to the dance floor to join the other couples that were already dancing. His arms were strong around me and cradled my already emotionally torn body to his and shielded me from any pain and hurt that was trying to destroy me. As the song ended he gently kissed my temple and whispered:

"Don't worry; everything is going to be alright. I'm right here for you." With that said he lead me back to the booth, and waived to Sheila to bring another drink for us along with a bowl of popcorn.

After Sheila left our drinks and popcorn, I decided I had to explain to Jeff why I was here and why I was so emotional about everything I saw.

"Jeff, I think I owe you an explanation. Tonight is very hard for me. I have not been out with anyone for almost twenty years. You see . . . I'm married."

I paused, waiting for a comment from Jeff, but continued when he did not say anything.

"I didn't have vacation time coming; I called in with an emergency leave from work, packed my bags and ran away from home. Wow, when I say it, I sound so foolish, ran away from home, this is something a teenager does. I have been so unhappy for the last few years. I feel trapped between a marriage that has gone stale, along with the responsibilities I feel towards my children. I seem to be living my life for everyone but myself. I am weepy, depressed, I just had to leave. I'm sorry; I shouldn't be here with you." I got my purse in hand, grabbed my jacket and stood up to leave. Jeff grabbed my hand as I moved past him and held it tight in his hand.

"Marilyn, please don't leave. We are just friends and if I can help I want to. When you want to leave I'll take you back, but don't walk out now. I can be a good friend."

I looked back at Jeff, and saw the sincerity in his eyes. It would be nice to have someone I could trust to talk to, I did want to stay. I felt drawn to Jeff, and it felt good to have someone want you to stay.

We stayed at The Office for quite a while talking about everything. I learned that Jeff was married once to his high school sweetheart. She was in a car accident while he was across country making a delivery in his truck. By the time he got word of the accident she had died. He didn't have time to see her one last time, and he will always regret not taking her in his arms and telling her how much he loved her before he left. He always felt she knew it so he didn't have to say it. He still lives with this guilt.

"Eleven thirty? I really have to get going Jeff. I'm glad I stayed. You are a wonderful person, and I hope you find that extra special girl you are looking for. You won't have to settle for anything less, you are worth the wait."

Jeff stood and helped me on with my jacket. As we walked out of the bar, Sheila waved good-bye, but I knew she wasn't waving at me. I saw a little twinge of jealousy in her eye as Jeff placed his hand at the small of my back again guiding me to the door.

Jeff said good-bye to everyone, and we were out the door walking back to my room.

"I can't tell you how much I have enjoyed this evening Marilyn."

"I did too Jeff. It was as if I have known you all of my life."

"I know, I felt the same way."

"Thank you Jeff."

"For what?"

"For not being too shocked when I told you about my family."

"I can't say I was surprised, but knowing as much about you as I do in this short time, I know what you did wasn't easy, and it wasn't done hastily."

All the lights at the café were out. The night cleaners were through and only the café light shone a light pink glow over the parking lot.

"Marilyn, one last thing; don't be too hard on your self, but give yourself some time before you make your decision."

Jeff then put his hand to my chin and lifted it to him. He gently lowered his lips to mine and then slowly kissed them.

"Have a good night. I will see you tomorrow."

Chapter 12

"Good morning Bob."

"Good morning Carey." Carey. A good secretary, very attractive, always second guessing my moods and my wants. Just wait she'll be walking in my office with a cup of coffee in hand.

"I thought you might like a cup of coffee this morning. I also stopped by the donut shop and brought a couple donuts for you. I hope you don't mind, you have been so preoccupied these past few days, I figured the privacy of your office is better than the break room."

"You always seem to know me better than I do myself Carey, thanks. The coffee was thoughtful, but the donuts are a real surprise. A nice one thanks again. I don't know what I would do without you."

"I hope you never try Bob."

As she turned and walked away I thought how lucky I was to have a secretary so in tune to me that she was able to second guess my needs. It has never been more important to me than now. I feel lost in my own world of business and my world of being an only parent. The pressure of both was beginning to wear on me, even though it has only been two days.

"Bob, here is your schedule for today. You have a meeting with the Blairs at 10:00 AM. They are here for a preliminary application for their new apartment complex. I have their file here. They have the land purchased; they're to bring in the plans and final bids today. At noon you have your monthly Chamber of Commerce meeting. Joe called to ask if you could take over the meeting as he has a family emergency. No need to call him if you can handle it, only if you can't. At two o'clock you will be meeting with the City Council to review the new business that wants to come into town. In this folder I have the EPA guidelines they have yet to comply with, along with a report on the plant they opened in Georgia three years ago. It looks like a clean plant with no complaints filed."

"Thanks again. That seems to be all I am saying to you today, but I mean it. I can use the extra attention now days."

Carey closed the door behind her and sat down in the chair in front of my desk.

"Bob, I don't want to pry, but I can't help noticing how distressed you have been. We have worked together a long time; I hope you realize I'm a friend if you want to talk. I'll always be here for you."

"Tell me something Carey; you were married once, what caused your break up?"

"Wow that was so long ago, almost five years now. Bill and I had been married about thirteen years. I had become a housewife, a chauffeur, a second mother to his kids, a maid, and any other servant you could think of. Whenever I would try to talk to him he would be distracted by the TV or anything else he was doing. The one thing he wasn't doing was listening to me. I tried to go to counseling, but Bill didn't think it was necessary. If he would have just once complemented me like you do for the little things I do, it would have helped. But he never did. Finally I realized that life was too short to live where I wasn't appreciated."

"You mean you just walked away?"

"Not exactly, but it all added up to that."

"Are you ever sorry?"

"At first I was. Every happy family, every child I saw reminded me of what I had left. I had no choice; if I was to survive I had to leave. Now, I still see the children, they aren't mine biologically, but I still love them like they are. They are doing fine, and we have a great relationship."

"And Bill?"

"We see each other occasionally. He still doesn't understand why I left, but he is living with someone else now, and seems very happy."

"And what about you?"

"I am still looking for my knight in shining armor, but all the knights I know are taken. Is everything alright with you and Mary?"

"Not exactly; when I got home Monday I found a note she had left. She left me Carey, and I honestly don't know why."

"What did she say in her note?"

"She said that she had to get away to decide what she wanted to do with her life, whatever that means. Suddenly I'm Mom and Dad, trying to hold everything together, while the kids think she is away at a friends helping out there."

"That's just like you Bob, covering for her and trying to do everything yourself."

"I don't know where to turn Carey. It seems that since Mary left, everything I do is wrong. I can't even give the kids lunch money without doing it wrong. Candy was telling me she had to have a new dress for a dance at school this week, and wants me to take her to the mall tonight. My God, she has more clothes in her closet now than she can possibly wear. When I tried to explain this to her she acted as if her whole world exploded."

"Bob do you mind a little friendly advice?"

"Please, I need anything friendly."

"Take Candy shopping. When you're a teenage girl everything that happens to you is dramatic, and a dance is especially so. If it is really true that she has so many clothes, then set a limit as to what she can spend, but first take the time to look at her clothes with her, and ask her what she has in mind. I think you will be surprised at her change of attitude. Give her some of your time, and it will work out."

"How did you become so smart?"

"Working for you; I have watched you with your employees, and this is exactly what you would do if someone requested something outside of their budget. You would ask them what they wanted, go over what they had, but most important, you would give them your time and attention. You would have come up with the same answer yourself, I know you."

"Thanks for the pep talk Carey, I really needed that."

"I wish I could be more help to you. You know where I am if you need me."

For the second time this morning Carey walked out of Bob's office, and for the second time this morning he felt a lot better about himself.

The day went by without him taking a break. He wasn't complaining, it's easier when he didn't have time to think about Mary. As he closed up his desk and put his coat on he decided he would take Carey's advice and take Candy shopping. He forgot how important dances can be when you are a teenager.

As he closed his office door, he noticed that almost everyone was gone, but Carey was still at her desk working as hard as she was when he came in this morning.

"Do you sleep here too?"

"No, I have some time to myself tonight, so I thought I would get a head start on tomorrow. It's better than sitting at home alone watching television."

"I tell you what. I have to pick the kids up from school after play practice, but I have about an hour and a half to kill, how about you joining me for a cup of coffee, maybe a piece of pie? It will give me a chance to pay you back for the donuts this morning."

"Bob, you don't have to pay me back, I was glad to do it, to be of some help."

"You were a great help, and I know I don't have to, I want to."

"I would love to Bob, thanks' for asking."

He helped Carey on with her coat after she had put everything away. As her hair brushed his hand he realized what a beautiful woman she is. He had always appreciated the way she had taken care of herself, and how attractive she was, but she was truly beautiful.

He noticed the looks from the other workers as they followed them as they walked out of the bank. He could remember giving others that same look whenever he saw two employees leaving work together, but this was different, and he resented their suspicions. They were friends, only friends, and he shouldn't have to apologize for having a cup of coffee with a friend. Don't they have anything better to do than to gossip about others?

"Bob, what is it?"

"Nothing worth talking about."

"It's the girls at the teller booths isn't it? Don't let it bother you; they check everyone out that leaves together. It doesn't bother me if it doesn't bother you."

"You saw them?"

"It happens every day; I'm surprised you haven't noticed before?"

"Let's get out of here. Can you follow me in your car, that way we can have a little more time before I have to leave to pick up the kids."

"Sure Bob, no trouble, no trouble at all."

It was nice to relax after work, and talk with someone that understood how he felt. Carey had listened to him talk this morning and never criticized him in his way of handling Candy, but instead gave him good, sound advice. He didn't ever remember her commenting on his personal life before, but perhaps he never shared anything with her before. It's funny how you can work with someone for a long time, and in an instant see her completely different.

"You are looking at me like you do when you are trying to size someone up before a meeting. Do I pass inspection or not?"

"I'm sorry; I'm realizing that I really don't know you at all. We have worked together for years, and all I know about you is what you have told me today. Oh, I know you are a great secretary, but I haven't learned much about you the person."

"What would you like to know?"

"Are you seeing anyone now?"

"No. Like I said earlier, all my knights in shining armor are taken."

"Then there is someone you are interested in?"

"I could be."

"Carey, you should tell him. I'm beginning to realize how suddenly things can change in your life. Maybe he feels the same about you. Who knows? All this time wasted without either one of you knowing how the other one feels."

"Someday maybe, but not now. The timings not right. Have you heard from Mary since she left?"

I was suddenly reminded of the pain I had been feeling all day about my own situation. I had managed to push it to the back of my mind, but Carey's concern had brought everything into focus again.

"No, I haven't heard a thing. I don't even know if she is safe or not. She said I shouldn't try to find her, that she will get back to me in a week. I will try and honor her wishes, but it's hard not knowing if she is alive or not."

"Bob, I'm sure she is fine. She apparently needs some time along, and this is the only way she knew how to get it."

"Do you understand her?"

"Bob, I feel so sorry for you." As she placed her hands over his Carey said, "Mary obviously doesn't know what she has left behind."

"The more I think about it the angrier I get. I have to take care of everything and she is out there trying to get herself together. What a cop-out. I can't understand anyone leaving their family like she did if she really cared."

"I can't either Bob. I wish there was something else I could say to help, but I don't understand her actions either. Was this all a surprise to you?"

"I was shocked!" I didn't have any idea she felt so troubled. Oh sure, she would make comments about how she felt, that she didn't have a life of her own, how I always came first with everything I did or wanted to do."

"Was she right?"

Bob was startled by her question. He had never felt that he had taken advantage of Mary.

"No, I don't think so. My work has to come first in my life; after all I am the one that supports my family. I came home after work, I never go out with the boys, or stop for drinks after work. I don't know what she has to complain about. I have always been faithful to her and gave her a beautiful house to live in. No, I haven't always come first; in fact my family has always been first."

"Do you honestly want to discuss this, I mean, do you want my opinion, a woman's opinion no matter how angry you might get? You know how I can sometimes be brutally honest."

"Yes, I would like to know your opinion. I value your judgment." That was one of the valuable things about having Carey as his secretary; she was able to analyses a situation and gives him her opinion, not what she thought he wanted to hear.

"All right, first your job, yes it does have to come first. Mary has a good job, but I'm sure your family depends on your income. I don't know too much about your friends, but

I do know that you belong to a golf league; you even travel in the winter to areas that have a golf course for a vacation. You also belong to many community organizations. I realize that this is a part or your job, as a bank vice president, you are expected to be a major contributor in the community, but let me play the devils advocated, how many nights a week are you gone to these meetings?"

"Maybe two, three tops."

"And then how many nights are you gone playing golf?"

"Two nights."

"Are these league nights?"

"Yes."

"And then, what if anyone asks you to play golf?"

"Sometimes I might play and extra night or two." He was starting to get a little irritated. After all he was the one that worked hard all day for his family. He worked his way up through the ranks. He wasn't related to the president of the bank, he had to prove himself, and he did it by hard work and long hours. He should be able to enjoy himself without being questioned about it.

"Bob, I can tell you are losing patients with me, but I told you, I am going to play the devil's advocate. If you aren't ready for this just tell me."

"No, you're right, I asked for your advice, continue."

"You are usually at the office long before anyone else arrives, you work a long day, and then you often have a meeting in the evening. What are you home long enough for, maybe eat and read a little of the paper? Then off to your meeting? If you don't have a meeting you are probably playing golf, or going to the club for exercise. What time are you usually home?"

"I'm always home by ten."

"You say that like you are proud of it. Bob, don't you see, Mary may not be the major bread winner of the house, but she has become the major caretaker of your home. She is the one that has taken care of your house, your children and of our needs. All the things that you resent right now, the responsibility of taking care of the children, putting their needs first, these are the things that Mary has been doing all along. If anything I'm sure that she feels like she is last on your priority list."

Bob was amazed at what she said. These were almost the exact words Mary had used, only for some reason tonight they made sense. He had put his committees, his golf and his job ahead of my family. It was convenient to have Mary do all the running, all the PTA meetings, the teacher's conferences, he was always unavailable.

"Why hadn't she explained all this to me? All she had to do was tell me?"

"I have a feeling that she did tell you, maybe many times, sometimes it takes someone outside the family to explain it a little clearer. Can I ask you a question, something you may not want to answer?"

"Sure."

"Is Mary involved with anyone else?"

"Mary? No, I'm sure she isn't."

"Good, that makes things easier for you."

"Why? What do you mean?"

"You have to decide if you want to change your life. If Mary decides that she can't continue to live the way she has, you will then be faced with the decision to change your patterns or you may be facing a divorce. Bob . . . Bob are you listening to me?"

"Yes, I heard you. Something you mentioned earlier, you asked if Mary was involved with anyone else. Why did you ask that? Have you heard anything about her and someone else?"

"Bob, no, I asked it because I needed to find out if there was another reason for her leaving."

"That would explain it. Of course, Mary is involved with someone. Why else would she leave her family?"

"Bob didn't you hear anything I said?"

"Yes I did, but that isn't enough reason to leave your husband and your children. It has to be another man, maybe she is out there seeing if she is attractive to other men. She is probably in a bar right now seeing the reaction other men will have to her. It makes me so angry to realize how little our family means to her."

"Bob, you don't really think Mary is doing these things, do you?"

"I don't know Carey; I only know that she has the opportunity, with no strings attached. It would be hard not to be fascinated with Mary. Besides being attractive, she has an honest quality that not many others have. It won't take long for the wolves to come out of the closet when they see her, and maybe that is what she wants. She can look around and take her choice of anyone, and if by chance she doesn't like what she sees, then she can come back home to us, and we are suppose to take her back just like that. Well, I've got news for her, it doesn't work that way."

"Do you really mean what you're saying?"

"Carey, I'm sorry. Don't listen to me tonight I don't know how I feel. I'm tired, depressed, and nothing makes sense to me anymore."

"How would you like to get out of here and come over to my place? We can have a drink, listen to music, talk if you like, or just sit and relax.

"I wish I could, it sounds great, but I have to pick up the kids, and I better go now. They'll be waiting for me. Thanks Carey thanks for being here for me tonight."

"Anytime you need someone to talk to, remember I'll be here for you . . . anytime."

Chapter 13

As I closed the door behind me, I felt a strange feeling sweep over me. I had felt comfortable all night with Jeff. He talked to me, listened to me, and for a short time, made me forget the mess my life was in.

But then, when he said good-bye, his kiss, what did he mean by that?

Oh, don't be so foolish Mary. He was being like a big brother. He hadn't stepped out of line all evening, and he could have, as emotional as I was tonight. He truly is a good friend.

Suddenly the telephone rang.

Who could that be? No one knows where I am?

"Hello?" I answered cautiously.

"Marilyn?"

"Jeff, is that you?"

"Yes. I wanted to thank you again for tonight. I also have a suggestion."

"A suggestion; what do you mean?"

"Why don't you give your husband a call? You can check on the kids, and maybe the two of you can iron out your differences. At least you can let him know you are safe so he won't have to worry so much."

"I'm not sure he's worrying."

"Marilyn, I am sure he *is* worrying. I know I would be if you walked out of my life. Call him. Give him a chance."

"Maybe . . . I'll have to think about it. Jeff?"

"Yes?"

"Thank you. I don't know what I would have done without you being so understanding tonight. I'll never forget it."

"You call home, and then get a good night's sleep. I'll see you first thing tomorrow. Good night Marilyn. Sleep tight.

"Jeff . . . my name's Mary, Mary Knutson. Good night."

When I hung up the telephone, I didn't want to let go of the receiver. I felt closer to Jeff just by keeping it in my hands.

Call home. I don't know if I can do that tonight. I wonder what Bob's reaction will be? I wonder what he has told the kids. Do they know the truth, or did he tell them the story I suggested? Maybe Jeff is right, maybe I should call him.

I cautiously took the receiver in my hand and slowly dialed the number.

My stomach was tied in knots as the telephone rang. Was I making a mistake calling so soon? What would I say if Bob wanted me to come home now, I'm not ready for that?

"Hello?"

"Bob? It's Mary."

There was no answer on the other end. I didn't say anything immediately, not knowing what to say.

"Bob?"

"Yes, I'm here."

"I thought I better call to let you know I'm okay."

"Where are you?"

"In a small town not too far away."

"Where Mary, where are you?"

I could tell his temper was getting the best of him with the impatience showing in his voice.

"Does it really matter?"

"No I guess it doesn't. You can be with your boyfriend anywhere we aren't known, can't you."

"Boyfriend . . . what are you talking about?"

"That is what this is all about isn't it? You have found someone else? Well, how does it feel to be out on the town with someone else? Is it as good as you thought it was going to be? Or is that why you are calling, you have decided you are coming back? Well, let me tell you something Mary, I don't know if I want you back."!

"You would think that wouldn't you. I have tried to tell you over the years that things weren't right between us and you never listened. I thought that if I left maybe, just maybe, you might begin to understand. All you can think about is that there must be another man. Nothing is ever wrong with you. Well I'm telling you, and it may be for the last time, you are wrong! There is something wrong with you, and for the first time I finally realize it's not with me. But I guess that is too much for you to understand isn't it Bob?"

"What do you want Mary?"

"I wanted to call and let you know I was okay and not to worry, but I was mistaken this time. You weren't worrying, you don't even care. Good night Bob."

With that I hung up the telephone and could feel the pain ebb over me again, only tonight with a feeling that was pulling me down into the depth of my despair, and this time, this time, there wasn't anyone around to help pull me up. I'm alone, all alone.

As the sun peeked through my curtains, I woke to a knocking at my motel room door.

"Marilyn, its Dolly, are you okay in there?"

"Dolly? What's the matter?"

"Hon, it's almost 9:30, I was afraid that you were ill or something. You didn't show up by 8:00, and I was concerned."

I opened the door to show Dolly I was okay.

"I'm sorry Dolly; I must have forgotten to set my alarm last night when I came in."

"Oh Hon, are you sure you're alright? You look like you have been crying all night."

I remembered my telephone call, and the emotional mess I was in. I was sure my eyes told the ending of my tale.

"I'm fine Dolly. Can you give me a little time to get myself together? I promise I'll be right over."

"Take all the time you need. I'm just glad you are okay." As Dolly turned to go back to the café she stopped and turned to add, "Oh by the way, Jeff was in for his coffee this morning. He was quite concerned that you didn't show up for work. He said that he would call you later."

"Thanks Dolly." I could see the questioning in her eyes, but I wasn't up to explaining the friendship that was developing between Jeff and me. And knowing Dolly she wouldn't ask me to explain. "I'll be in as soon as I can."

I couldn't believe I had forgotten to set the alarm last night. I knew I was upset after talking to Bob, but I am usually not so distracted.

Bob, he would think I was having an affair with someone. I think he loves me in his own way, but he has always been so possessive he has never been comfortable with me having friends, certainly not male friends.

I thought this time away from him would give him time to think about our problems as well as me, but now I can see the only thing he is thinking about is my infidelity. Perhaps my leaving has made things worse. He certainly sounded furious on the telephone. What did I expect? I knew he would be mad when he found the note, but I never expected him to think that I was unfaithful. How could he think that of me.? His words last night hurt me more than any he had spoken in the past. They were like knives severing any threads of hope that were holding our marriage together. I know now that I can't continue with this marriage. I have taken too much hurt, too many nights of being alone, and too many nights of tears to want it to continue.

It has been so long, I can't even remember the last time Bob and I had a night to ourselves. He was always too busy with his committees and his golfing to remember he had a wife at home. Over the past years, I can't remember anything worth holding our marriage together, except for the children.

Rob and Candy, how would I explain this to them? They were both teenagers, old enough to understand, or were they?

You always hear that children never understand divorce, and they always want to see their parents back together, will they understand that I have to leave Bob to keep my own sanity?

What will happen to me if I stay in a marriage that has died? I need Rob and Candy to understand. They are the only reason worth living. They are the glue that holds my marriage together. They are my reason for getting up in the morning. I know I felt like a chauffeur at times, but I also know that they appreciated everything I did for them. They knew they could count on me, and I tried to be there for them. My kids mean the world to me, and until they are out of high school, they will be my priority in life. I will make our lives as normal as possible, but I have made my decision. When I go back home, I will see a lawyer. I can't continue my life as I have, being married to Bob.

"Sorry about this morning Dolly. It won't happen again."

"That's OK Marilyn; I handled it with no problem. Now, how are you?"

"Me? I'm fine."

"Really . . . how are you? You looked terrible this morning."

"Last night I called my husband to see how he and the kids were, and to let him know I was alright. Do you know what he wanted to know?"

"Sit down Hon; I can see this is upsetting you all over again. Now, what did he say?"

"He wanted to know if I was enjoying this time with my boyfriend. If it was as good as I thought it was going to be. Can you believe that? I hate him Dolly. I can't believe he would say such a thing to me. I'll never forgive him for that."

"Wow, why would he say such a thing?"

"Dolly, I have never been unfaithful to him, never!"

"I didn't mean that you had Hon, I just wondered where he came up with an idea like that. Has he ever accused you of that before?"

"No."

"Marilyn, now don't make any hasty decisions. He was probably angry and said things that I am sure he is sorry for now. Give it time. A marriage is something you can't end hastily."

"I know that Dolly, that's why it has taken me years to get this far. I couldn't even let myself take the time to assess everything until this year. I have always come last in my life, and I want to be first or at least a place above the laundry or the dishes. I have to matter, not only to me but to my family too."

"You sit down here and have a cup of coffee. I have a couple of things to do out back. Now you relax, we have time before the lunch crowd comes in."

"Thanks Dolly. I don't know what I would do without you."

When the telephone rang, Dolly yelled from the kitchen:

"Can you get that for me Hon?"

"Sure Dolly. Dolly's Café."

"Marilyn? I mean Mary?"

Love is like a Butterfly

"Jeff, hi, how are you?"

"I'm fine, but the question is how are you? Dolly said you didn't show up for work this morning. I was afraid that you decided to leave and go back home."

"Nothing as dramatic as that; I must have forgotten to set my alarm last night, and I slept in."

"Did you end up calling Bob last night?"

"Say, where are you calling from?"

"Milwaukee. I am waiting for my truck to be unloaded. Then I will have one more stop before heading for home. I'll stop by the café for some coffee, and then maybe we can make plans."

"Make plans? What are you talking about?"

I'm talking about tonight. Don't plan anything; I think you need someone to talk to again."

"Jeff, I can't unload to you all the time. I'm sure you have more important things to do than baby-sit me."

"You know, I can't think of one thing right now. Don't argue. Besides, I want to see you. I have been thinking about you all day. Don't say no. It won't be anything fancy, just a pizza or a show. I'll be home about 7:30 and I'll pick you up at 8:00."

He waited for an answer, and I struggled with myself typing to decide what I should do. I wanted to meet him tonight. It did feel nice to have someone to talk to, someone that didn't judge me, but I was concerned about the kiss he gave me. True, it was platonic, but I'm not going to complicate my situation with an involvement with another man. I was still married, even though my marriage was over.

73

"Mary? Say yes. Don't worry, I know you are married, and I admire your commitment to it. You won't get any complications from me, only friendship."

"Thanks Jeff, I appreciate your understanding, and yes, I would love to have a pizza with you tonight."

"Great! See you then."

As I hung up the telephone I could feel a wave of relief flood over me. It was as if a load had already been lifted. I had a good friend, and somehow just talking to him made the day ahead a little more bearable."

"Anything important on the telephone?"

"No just Jeff checking to see if everything was okay."

"Jeff? Is there something special developing there?"

"Only a special friendship Dolly, nothing more."

"Good. Don't get me wrong, Jeff is a great guy, but I don't think you need any involvement at this time."

"No, what I have needed is a husband that loves me, but instead I have lived with a man that I thought I knew, but now find out he is only a stranger, and a stranger that has a cruel streak in him waiting to strike out at me."

The tears started to stream down my face again. I had felt that I had decided to end this marriage, but if that is true, why the tears? It's over, and it is what I want. Oh, I wish I could control my tears; I get so mad at myself for being so weak. Why can't I be strong like Bob?

Chapter 14

"Good morning Bob, how are you today?"

"Oh, Carey . . . good morning."

"When did you come in today? It's only 7:30 now."

"I was here about six. I woke up and couldn't get back to sleep. The kids had to be at school early, so they were up too. No reason to stay at home, I thought I might as well get a head start on today."

"Let me get you some coffee."

"Thanks Carey. You sure take good care of me."

"It's my pleasure Bob, you know that."

As Carey turned to get coffee for Bob, her mind wandered back to the day she was hired. She was well qualified, but a number of the men didn't want her as their secretary. She was too pretty, too shapely, and dressed too classy. I suppose their wives would have objected. Bob didn't stop to think twice. He looked at her resume and told personnel he would be glad to have someone with her qualifications working on his team. He never considered her his secretary, but part of his team. She had this problem before, but from that day on, she promised herself he would never be sorry. She would work hard and long for him, and it wasn't long before everyone saw what a good employee she was. She was always on time, most of the time early, and she always seemed to be one step ahead of Bob, she would continually have just the right papers pulled from the file for him to review.

Then one day it started the gossip. It was probably started by one of the other secretaries that were jealous of her, but every time she was in Bob's office a little longer than usual, or whenever she would bring a sandwich back from her lunch hour because Bob was too busy to take a break, she could feel the eyes watching her. Finally the rumors got back to Bob. That was the day he called her into his office.

"Carey, we need to talk. You know how pleased I have been with your work this past year don't you?"

"Yes, I think I do." I had no idea what this was all about.

"The word has gotten back to me that we are seeing each other, socially."

"Bob that's not true, you know it isn't."

"Yes, of course I do. I shouldn't have to ask you this, but you know Mary. We have been married almost ten years now, and she is the best thing that has happened to me. I will never do anything that would compromise my marriage."

"Bob, I'm sorry this has happened, but have I ever done anything out of line?"

"No you haven't, that is why I am talking to you. I have already talked to Mary to understand her feelings. If she felt threatened by you, then I would relocate you within the bank. I have assured her that there is nothing between us, and she believes me."

"Thank you."

"Now, we have to deal with these people that are intent on spreading rumors about us. Whenever I stay in my office because I am too busy for lunch, I am going to have to ask you not to bring me anything. We will have to watch our casual talking and keep everything to business. It won't be too long until everything will die down, and we can get back to normal, but until then, I have to ask you to bear with me. I don't want to lose you, but my position is too important to let a few loose tongued women destroy all I have worked for."

"Bob I will do anything you say and thank you for having enough confidence in me to put up with this."

As she left his office, she was furious. Why is it people don't have anything better to do than to make up stories about others, and that is what it was, all stories. Yes, she did go out of her way for Bob, but it was all professional. There were many times she wished it were more than that, but as Bob said, he loved his wife, and that came first.

She could never picture them together. She had seen Mary at the office parties, and she was nice, a hometown girl, but she had no style, no sparkle. That didn't seem to make a difference to Bob. He should have a wife with flair that every other man would be envious of. There were many times she would be embarrassed for him by the comments Mary would make, but he would only hug her and give her a kiss on the cheek. Bob deserved more; someone in his position should have a wife that he would be proud to take with him. She had worked for Bob now for almost ten years. Every day she could picture herself next to Bob and the children instead of Mary. She would be able to help direct his career. She would be able to entertain and make Bob proud of every move she made. She deserved it. She understood him. Yes, he is the one she was in love with, my knight in shining armor, but it is too soon to let him find out. The timing isn't right. She will be here for him every day, and if the opportunity arises, she will be there to pick up the pieces, but she must be careful and wait. Bob finally depends on her, and she had to make sure that dependency grew.

"Here's your coffee Bob. Do you need to talk?"

"You know me better than anyone don't you?"

"Yes, I think I do. You are very special to me. You're not only my boss but you are my best friend too."

"Thanks Carey, it's good to have someone to confide in. Mary called last night."

"Really . . . how nice, has she changed her mind about staying away?" Carey thought she sounded a little too cheery trying to hide her disappointment and near panic.

"No, she wanted me to know she was okay."

"How did you react to that?"

"I asked her how it felt to be away from home with her boyfriend."

"You asked her that?"

"Yes, after talking with you I realized that there must be someone else involved with her. That is why she left. I was so angry it came tumbling out without thinking, but I'm not sorry I said it."

"Did she admit it?" Carey said, as she secretly crossed her fingers.

"No, she denied it and hung up on me."

"Did you expect her to admit it?"

"I'm not sure what I expected. It all happened so fast I don't think either one of us thought about it."

Carey got up from her chair in front of Bob's desk and walked behind Bob, and started to gently rub his shoulders.

"Bob, I'm so sorry. If there is anything I can do, please ask. Mary must be the craziest person on earth to give you up for someone else. I'll never understand her."

Carey left Bob's office with a new agenda on her mind. All this time she had been the trusty secretary, his right hand, but now she had an opportunity to become more, something that she had wanted for a long time. This would take careful planning, and she couldn't make any mistakes.

Bob dug into his work this morning and Carey worked just as hard making sure everything went smoothly. The telephone had been unusually quiet today, and Carey jumped as it rang and broke her concentration.

"Bob Knutson's phone", she answered.

"Carey? This is Mary, is Bob in I have to talk to him."

"Bob? Is he in? Just a minute Mary." Now what do I do Carey thought as she covered the telephone with her hand. I can't let her talk to him; maybe she is trying to make up.

"Gee Mary; he just left for a meeting. Can I take a message or a number where he can reach you?"

"Is everything okay Carey?"

"Yes, why would you ask that?"

"Is Bob really in a meeting?"

"Mary, I don't want to be put in the middle of this, but Bob has left specific instructions that he doesn't want to talk to you."

"Well, you tell Bob I will talk to him sooner or later. I will call him tonight at home, around seven. Will you at least give him the message for me?"

"Sure Mary, you know I'll do anything I can, we have been friends a long time, but Bob is my boss and I have to do as he says."

"I know. You have been a good friend, just tell Bob I called and I will call tonight. Thanks Carey, bye.

"Bye Mary." What a mess now what should she do? She had to think of something to keep Bob away from his house tonight.

"Mr. Knutson's phone."

"This is Mr. Williams' secretary. Mr. Williams would like bob to meet him in his office at 5:30 this evening."

Mr. Williams is the president of the bank; I wonder what he wants Carey wondered.

"I'll check his calendar, one moment please." This is the answer to a number of problems.

"I'm sorry, but Mr. Knutson has a late appointment at five thirty but he will be available at six thirty."

"Six thirty will be fine. Please have him meet Mr. Williams in the Board Room."

Now, Carey thought, I will have to handle everything else myself.

"Bob, Mr. Williams' secretary called and there is an important meeting he wants you to attend at six thirty in the Board Room.

"Carey, I can't meet with him then, I have to pick up the kids tonight from school, and I'll never be back in time."

"Bob, let me help you. I'll pick up the kids and take them home, and then I will wait there until you get home just to make sure everything is okay."

"I can't ask you to do that, you have your own life to live, I can't have you running interference for me at home as well as at the office."

"Nonsense; I have nothing else planned tonight, and besides, I haven't seen Candy in a long time. Maybe we can have a girl chat."

"Okay you win, but the first night I have free I will pay you back by taking you to dinner, and I won't take no for an answer."

The rest of the afternoon went by slowly for Carey. Every time she looked at the clock it seemed to have moved only a few minutes. Finally it was closing time, and she quickly put everything on her desk away, and checked in with Bob one last time before leaving.

"Bob, I'm leaving now. I'll pick Candy up at school at six o'clock and take her home. I'll wait until your meeting is over; don't worry about the time as I don't have anything on tonight."

"There's no need for you to wait, Candy can stay by herself."

"No really, I want to. Let me do this for you."

"Thanks Carey you're a life saver."

Carey drove aimlessly around town, killing time until it was time to pick up Candy. She tried to plan what she should be doing to endear herself to Bob, but nothing sensible came to mind. She would just continue to be available and helpful whenever she could.

Carey saw Candy as she pulled up in front of the school. She was struck by the resemblance of Mary in her. Her carefree attitude while with her friends gave her an air of confidence that was always lacking in Mary. It was easy to see that Candy's friends considered her important by the way she caught everyone's attention while talking. Carey drove slowly to the group, and rolled down the window to talk to Candy.

"Candy, is that you?"

"Hi", Candy responded as she leaned over to look into the car.

"Do you remember me? I'm Carey, you Dads secretary."

"Oh sure; hi again. Its been awhile since I saw you, last year at the picnic I think."

"You're right, you have a good memory. Candy, your Dad had an emergency meeting with Mr. Williams. He asked me if I could stop by and get you, and then wait until he comes home. Do you have to give anyone else a ride home?"

"No, not tonight," Candy said as she got into the car. "Do you know the way to my house?"

"Yes . . . oh, well, your Dad gave me the instructions, and I drove past it before coming after you. I always like to know what directions I'm going."

Candy noticed the little fluster that occurred in Carey's voice when asking if she knew where they lived. Why would anyone get flustered at a simple question like that?

"Thanks for picking me up Carey, since Mom is out of town, Dad has the job of running with Rob and I, and I don't think he appreciates it."

"Why is your Mom out of town again?" Carey asked.

"She went to visit a friend that needed her."

"That sounds strange doesn't it, just to pick up and leave on a moment's notice?"

"Strange?" Not for Mom. She is available for anyone who needs her. She has a lot of friends."

"Oh I'm sure she has, it seemed strange to me that she wouldn't have taken your family into consideration first, but I imagine you are used to that. I understand your mother puts in a lot of hours at the insurance office."

"Yes, she has lately, but she was filling in for someone that needed the time off." Candy looked at Carey with a suspicious concern now. She had never heard Carey say anything negative about her mother, but tonight she was making innuendoes ever since she picked her up.

"I give your mother a lot of credit. She has a full time job, works extra hours, does running for you kids and Bob, and still finds time for her own needs, and friends." I have to be careful not to be too critical of Mary, Carey thought. I have to make Candy my friend.

"Candy, I hope you don't mind, but I was talking to your father the other day, and I explained how important it is for a teenage girl to have a new outfit for dances. I wasn't trying to interfere, but I did think it was important."

"You talked to Dad? I wondered what changed his mind in such a hurry. No, I'm not mad, I'm glad you did."

As they drove into the driveway, Carey glanced at her watch and noticed it was 6:45; Mary would be calling in about fifteen minutes. How would she handle that?

"Candy, I told your Dad I would stay until he got home tonight. I also have had some calls transferred to your house, I hope you don't mind. I brought some work home with me, and I need to get some information straight. Do you mind if I answer the telephone tonight for about a half hour?"

"No, I don't care. I have homework to do anyway, so you can have some privacy in the den."

As they entered the house, Carey was taken aback by how lovely it was. The living room was very formal, and you could tell it was used for special occasions and for entertaining. The carpet and furniture were done in tones of beige. The walls exhibited a carefully matched collection of original paintings. Bob had mentioned that Mary had started collecting prints and oils years ago. It was obvious that Mary had a knack in recognizing early talent. The kitchen and dining area gave a warm glow of welcome. There was a counter with stools for quick snacks or a lunch, but also a dining area for a family meal. A small desk in the corner by the telephone made business conversations easier to handle with pen and paper nearby.

The den was very masculine. Large overstuffed furniture beckoned, and one could become lost in the softness of its cushions. The fireplace looked as if it was used often. Wood was stacked next to it in a hodge-podge way, and the grate had ashes piling under it. There was a beautiful wood shelving unit that housed a television, DVD player, and a stereo unit with large speakers. Track lighting could be placed anywhere around the room to give just the right lighting wherever needed. Carey noticed a telephone in the den next to the chair she imagined to be Bobs. It felt right to be sitting in the chair that he had sat in only hours before.

Suddenly the telephone rang. Carey immediately grabbed it so that Candy would not answer. Changing her voice so that it could not be recognized, she answered:

"Hello."

"Hello, is this the Knutson's?"

"Yes it is, who is this?" It was Mary on the other end. Carey still hadn't decided what she would say, but she was very good at ad-libbing.

"Is Bob there? May I speak to him?"

"Bob? Oh no," giggle, giggle, "he's in the shower now, but I can take a message."

"Who is this?"

"Me? I'm Bonnie Sue, who's this?"

"I'm Mary, Bob's wife."

"Oh, Mary, Bob told me about you a long time ago, hi."

"I'm sorry, you have me at a disadvantage, Bob didn't tell me about you."

"Well that naughty boy, we've known Bob for a long time. We meet him golfing, and we have gotten together ever since."

"We?"

"Yes, me and my twin sister Connie. She made his favorite chili for him tonight, and we thought we would make it a threesome."

"Chili?"

"He absolutely loves her chili; she puts cheese on top of hers. You should try it sometime; Bob really loves it that way."

"Just how long have you known Bob?"

"Just a minute Bob, I'll be right there. I'm sorry, Bob needs his . . . well, his back washed, but I'll tell you what, I'll tell Bob you called, and he can give you a call when we're, oh, when he's done."

Suddenly the telephone line went dead, and then the dial tone rang in Carey's ear.

"I wonder if she could tell it was me. I don't think so. One thing for sure, I won't have to worry if Mary will try to get back with Bob. Now, all I have to do is to be here for him. I will be. No matter if it is night or day.

Chapter 15

"Dolly, is Marilyn around?"

"Jeff, come on over here a minute."

Dolly called Jeff over to a quiet corner of the café where she could talk privately to him.

"Jeff, I know that you were planning on meeting Marilyn tonight, but something has come up, and she asked me to tell you she will see you tomorrow."

"What happened Dolly?"

"Nothing Jeff, give her some time, she will be all right."

"Dolly, what's going on?"

"I shouldn't be telling you this, but knowing you, you'll run right over to her room if I don't explain. Marilyn called her husband at work today, and Bob had left word with his secretary that he didn't want to talk to her. Then around seven this evening she called him at home. She was determined to find out if he really meant what he said the other night. Anyway, when she called, a strange woman answered, and I guess he had some kind of party going on, you know the kind, two women and one man. She knew Mary's name and everything, even the food that Bob liked. Seems these women have known him for quite a while.

Mary feels like the rug has been pulled out from under her. She doesn't have a thread left of her marriage to hold on to anymore. She needs some space, and a lot of time to cry. Jeff, I want you to give that time to her. If you care at all you'll do that.

"How could he do something like that?"

"I don't know. In the short time I have known Marilyn I really like her. To be honest, I don't know if she can take much more. When she left home she was depressed, and unable to cope any longer. I don't know what last nights experience will do to her."

"It's good she has you Dolly. She needs you now more than ever."

"You are important to her too Jeff. After you called and told her that you were taking her out for pizza tonight, it was the first time all day I saw a smile on her face."

Dolly turned from Jeff as if biting her lip not to continue.

"Dolly, what is it?"

"Jeff honey, you know how much I care about you, but I would hate to see you become involved with Marilyn now. She is so disturbed by her own situation I don't think she could handle anything else."

"Dolly, I know you said that for Marilyn's benefit, but you didn't have to. Ever since my wife died I haven't even given another woman a second glance. Marilyn is different. Not in a romantic sense, but more as a soul mate. I care what happens to her, and that concern has become an all-consuming fire in me. For the first time in years I have met someone that is honest and kind, and no matter what it takes, I will make sure that her husband realizes what he has lost. And you know that smile you saw on her face this afternoon? Well, get used to it, because you will be seeing a lot of it from now on."

With that said, Jeff turned and walked out of the café. Not in a slow methodical walk, but more like a man with a purpose. A man on a mission that couldn't be diverted.

Chapter 16

Carey sat in Bob's chair calming herself after her telephone conversation with Mary. It felt right to be in Bob's chair. The massive leather chair surrounded her with softness, yet a strength that certainly fit Bob. All of this will be hers if she has the patience to wait and the ability to be creative. She had already proved she could be creative. Her conversation with Mary was not planned, however it flowed nicely. Mary would be convinced that Bob didn't miss her at all, but also that Bob had been occupied in the past with the sisters named Bonnie and Connie. She was sure that this was something that Mary could never forget or forgive.

What was that noise? It was the garage door opening, and that meant Bob was driving his car into the garage. Carey scrambled to get some papers out of her briefcase, and appeared to have been working for some time.

"Hi Carey; I told you you didn't have to wait until I got home, Candy can stay by herself."

"I know Bob, but I wanted to. Candy and I had a lovely talk on the way home. You have done a wonderful job of raising her. She has your common sense and your good looks. It won't be long and she will have the boys beating down the doors."

"I know what you mean. They are already calling, and I don't think I am ready for that."

He didn't even pick up on the compliment that I thought he was good looking, Carey thought. I don't want to be too obvious, but I want to make a move soon, or Mary will be back in town, and things won't be so easy then.

"I do appreciate your comments on how much Candy needed a new dress for the school dance. It still doesn't make sense to me, but that little gesture of taking her to the mall and agreeing on an outfit prevented a cold war around here."

So, all my trouble wasn't in vain, Carey was encouraged. First I made Candy aware that I was the one responsible for her getting her new outfit, and now Bob is thanking me for my advice. I think this is the way to get to him, through his children.

Just then Carey heard the front door open and someone come in. It had to be Rob. Bob didn't seem to notice. Now if she could time this right, it could also work for her benefit.

"Bob, do you mind one more piece of advice?" Carey asked as she scanned the dark hallway and could see Rob's shadow approaching the family room.

"I know that this is none of my business, but I think it is important that you tell the kids what is going on." Carey checked the hallway again out of the corner of her eye, and saw Rob stopped, watching and listening, and Candy coming out of her room to see what had caught Rob's attention.

"Carey, you know that I don't want to alarm them."

"I know that is what you said," Carey said in a slightly louder voice so that it could not be misunderstood, "but I have always felt that in any family the children are the most important. You and Mary can go on and live separate lives, but the children will always be affected by Mary's actions. I think that they should know that she left you to go running around with . . . who knows who. You are their anchor. You are the one that has stood by them. I don't see you abandoning them! They should realize which parent is the one they can depend on."

"Carey, we don't know . . ."

"Bob, we know Mary is gone, we know she left you a note, and we know that she has not gotten in touch with you as she said she would. She didn't give a second thought to you or the kids, only to herself." Carey had quickly interrupted Bob. She had to make sure the kids did not know that Mary was off by herself. "Think about it. The kids are old enough to understand, and I think you need their support now."

"I'm going to leave now, remember, if you need anything call me, even if you need to talk. I will drop anything for you or the kids; you should know that by now. Think about what I said."

"I don't know Carey, every instinct I have tells me to wait and not tell the kids, but I will think about it. Thanks for picking up Candy."

Carey slowly walked up to Bob and put her arms around him and gave him a gentle hug, holding onto him a little longer than she needed to.

"You'll make it through this. Hang in there."

As Carey left, Bob turned and collapsed in his chair. Could Carey be right? Should he tell the kids? Mary will call, she will. She loves me, I know she does.

"Dad? What's this about Mom? Where is she?"

"Rob? What do you mean? She's with Joan."

"Come on Dad, I overheard you and Carey talking. What note is she talking about? Is Mom involved with someone else?"

"Oh Rob, I'm sorry you heard that, it's nothing for you to worry about, Carey has an overactive imagination that's all."

"Daddy?" Candy slowly walked into the room with tears streaming down her face.

"Daddy, did Mom really leave us? Is she gone?"

Bob held out his arms to Candy and Rob and tried to surround them with his love and confidence. It was all he could do now. How could he explain Mary's actions when he didn't understand them himself?

"Daddy, I want to see the note. Please let us read it," Candy begged.

"Candy that won't solve anything; now, go finish your homework and let's call it a night."

"Dad, you can't treat us like little kids. We have heard this much, now you have to fill us in on the truth. Don't you see, not knowing is worse than anything you could tell us?"

Rob was right. They knew this much, they had to know the truth, or their imaginations would make up things.

Bob went to his room and retrieved the note Mary left from beneath his underwear. He had hidden the note to make sure that neither Candy nor Rob would find it accidentally.

As Candy read the note her tears started to roll down her cheeks. She had always been close to her mother, and she felt emptiness like she had never known before.

Rob took the note from Candy as she finished. As he read the note his face hardened and his jaw clenched as his face muscles jerked with the pressure of his teeth pressed tightly together. When he finished the note he handed it back to Bob, and the three of them sat in silence.

"Daddy, what does this mean? Doesn't she love us anymore?"

"Candy, you know your mother, how can you even ask a question like that? Of course she loves you. When a man and woman break up it isn't because they no longer love their children, it is because they are having trouble, she will always love you."

"Is that what is happening Daddy? Are you and Mom getting a divorce?"

"Candy, I didn't mean that, it was just a figure of speech. I don't know what your mother is thinking. I have only talked to her once, and that wasn't a very productive conversation."

"Productive conversation? Dad this isn't one of your meetings here. This is your marriage; this is our family you are talking about. What exactly did you say?

Rob had a way of cutting through the emotions and getting straight to the heart of things.

"She told me not to worry, that she was in a small town not too far away."

"Daddy, you didn't get mad at her did you? You didn't holler at her?"

"Candy, I didn't holler, but yes, I was upset, wouldn't you be?"

"What did you say Dad?"

Suddenly his accusations seemed harsher than they did as he was saying them to Mary. He was sure it was because he didn't want his children to have to deal with this, but they wanted to know the truth, and maybe Carey was right, they deserved to know.

"I can't remember exactly, but it was something like asking how it felt to be in another town with her boyfriend."

"Boyfriend? Daddy how could you."

"Candy, we don't know for sure where Mom is or if she is with anyone."

"Dad, what did she say to your questions?"

"She said that I would think of something like that. She said the problem was with me, but now that I think about it she never did deny it. She got mad at me and hung up."

"Oh Daddy, don't you see? All she wanted was for you to say you missed her and loved her, and what did you do? You accused her of being with a boyfriend. Men! Don't you ever think of anything else but yourself? Don't you see how much she must have been hurting to pack up and leave us all?"

As Candy talked, her quiet tears turned into mournful sobs. She loved her mother so much she couldn't; no she wouldn't see the disaster Mary had caused. She turned and ran into her bedroom slamming the door behind her. I could hear her sobs in the family room, but I was helpless. What could I say to ease her pain?

"Dad, is there another problem we don't know about? Is there something else between you and Mom?"

"Rob, I know you are trying to rationalize this, but believe me, I have been over and over it in my mind. We didn't have a big fight; everything has been the same as usual. I don't know what I could have done differently."

"It just doesn't make sense Dad."

"So what happens now?"

"We wait. I can't do anything until I hear from your mother again. Maybe next time she will tell me where she is."

"And then what? Will you tell her you love her, or is that all over?"

"Rob, I love your mother, I always will. Whatever made her think we had a problem is beyond me. Between you and me, I don't know what I would do without her, she is my support. I know I act strong, but I rely on your mother for so much."

"I think you are telling the wrong person Dad. You need to tell Mom this."

"Your mother already knows this."

"I think she needs to hear it from you."

Maybe Rob is right, maybe this is part of the reason Mary left. Could it be that after all these years she wasn't sure of his feelings? Didn't she know he couldn't live without her, that he can't even imagine trying? He knows one thing, he misses her terribly, and if this is what life without her would be, he didn't want another day of it.

Chapter 17

"Hi Sheila, this is Mary Knutson, is Randy in? Thank you."

This call to the family lawyer will be hard, but it is something I have to do.

"Randy, this is Mary Knutson; I have a big favor to ask you." As I talked tears welled up in my eyes, and I had to stop talking for a few minutes to regain my composure. I had thought about it all night, and there was no sense prolonging this. After my telephone call to Bob, and talking to whoever it was, it was clear to me that the reason I have felt so separated from Bob for all these years was because he had been seeing someone else, or many others. I find it hard to believe, but how can I argue with what I heard?

Randy, I'm sorry, what I have to ask you is very hard I know it may sound strange, but please don't question me."

"Mary, what is it?"

"I want you to file divorce papers for me. I want you to call Bob and tell him that I want a divorce and I will agree to no charges being filed against him just mutual consent. If he won't agree, then I will file, and he knows I have grounds."

"Mary, when did all this happen?"

"I'm out of town now, and I have finally put together the pieces of the puzzle, with the help of two, shall I say, ladies, that Bob was entertaining while I'm away. I have to make the break now Randy, my sanity depends on it."

"Mary, are you sure? This doesn't sound like Bob. Have you talked to him?"

"I tried, but he won't talk to me. I'm sure you won't have any trouble with him, he will be glad to get out of this marriage too. Now listen Randy, I trust you to do what has to be done. I will call back in a few days and find out what you need me to do. If you can, please file everything right away, now that I have made my decision, it seems to be very important that it is done quickly."

"Mary, I'm shocked! Give me your number and I will get back to you."

"Randy, I don't want anyone to know where I am. I'll call you."

"Mary, I'm your lawyer, everything you tell me is confidential, now give me your number and I will get back to you. I won't give this information to anyone, not even to Sheila; my secretary if that makes you feel safer."

"Alright Randy, I do trust you, but hurry; this has been a hard decision. My number is 897-4249, this is a café where I have been working the past few days, if I'm not there leave a message and I will call back. Remember, not a word to Bob where he can reach me."

"That's a midland number isn't it?"

"Yes, I started driving, and this is where I ended up, you know how they say you can't run away from your troubles? They are right, I brought them with me."

"Mary, are you okay? Is there anyone with you?"

"No, there isn't anyone with me, but I'm fine. I have met a few good people, and for the first time in my life I am finding out that I can manage by myself."

"Of course you can. You are a very strong person Mary Knutson, but please, take your time in making a final decision. I'll call in a few days and see if this is what you really want, and if it is, then we will proceed."

"No Randy, I have decided, start whatever has to be done, there is no sense waiting."

"Whatever you say."

"Thanks Randy, you are a good friend." As I hung up tears were falling again, but there was a strange sense of relief that came over me, along with a deep emptiness.

"Sheila, get me Bob Knutson at the National Bank."

Randy thought over the conversation he had just had with Mary. He had known Bob and Mary for years, and had been their lawyer for over ten years. Bob has always been the professional, chairing committees and active in civic activities. Mary was always the "little woman" waiting at home. She took good care of the kids and was always there for Bob. She was never out in the limelight, but always in the shadows supporting her family. He could not believe that Bob would jeopardize all he had for a life that could ruin his reputation.

"Randy, how are you? Say we haven't gotten together for golf this summer, I thought we were going to put our schedules aside and make this a priority?"

"You're right Bob, time seems to slip away without taking time for the important things."

"You don't sound too happy today, can I help with something?"

"Bob, I don't know how to say this, but I just got a call from Mary."

"You did? Did she say where she was?"

"Yes, as a matter of fact she did."

"Randy, I know you won't understand this, but I have to know where I can reach her, it's important."

"I'm sorry, I can't tell you that."

"What do you mean you can't tell me? Why did Mary call you?"

"She asked me to start divorce proceedings as soon as possible."

"Divorce proceedings!"

"I'm sorry Bob. She said that she would agree to mutual consent, but if you fought it she would file charges against you."

"Charges, against me? What charges?"

"Bob, maybe you should come over to my office and we can discuss this in person."

"No Randy, I need to know right now what she said."

"It had something to do with you entertaining two ladies while she was out of town."

"Randy that's plain crazy."

"Bob, I'm only telling you what she told me. Mary wants me to start proceedings immediately. I have to call her back and tell her your answer. Why don't you come over, we can talk, and try to make some sense of this."

"I'll be right over. Clear the rest of the day for me if you can, if you can't, I'll sit in your waiting room until you have time for me." With that said Bob hung up his telephone and sat in shock at his desk. Mary had gone away to clear her head, and now she is filling for divorce. None of this makes any sense.

Bob looked at his calendar for the day and saw that he had two appointments for this afternoon.

"Carey, please clear my calendar for the rest of the day. I have an emergency and I have to leave the bank."

"Is everything okay? Anything I can help with?"

"No, this I have to handle myself."

"Can I reach you someplace, in case of emergency?"

"No, I'll check back with you later." Bob answered as he pulled on his suit coat and walked out of his office.

Carey watched him as he quickly walked out of the bank without a look back. What was going on? Had he heard from Mary? Is that it, was he going to meet her?

There was no way that she could find out now, she would have to wait. Everything was going so perfectly, and now, what was happening?

Chapter 18

Bob walked into Randy's office and checked in with Sheila, his secretary. He had been in this office so many times before, and had always felt at home. Today it was as if he had entered Randy's office for the first time. Bob was walking in a fog unable to process anything, his steps, his actions happened without thought. It was like he was running on automatic pilot. How could Mary have thought that he was seeing anyone else?

Finally he heard Randy's secretary answer questions into her telephone. Bob knew she was talking to Randy.

"Yes, he's here. I was able to clear the next hour for you, but you have a meeting with Mr. Hill. He insists he could not be canceled. I'll send Mr. Knutson right in."

"Bob, Randy can see you now."

"Thanks Sheila."

As Bob walked down the hallway to Randy's office he was feeling exposed and vulnerable. He had never confided in anyone, except Carey, that there was ever a problem with him and Mary, and now he would have to be open and honest if he expected Randy to help him.

"Bob, come in, and shut the door behind you."

Bob walked in and sat in front of Randy. The chair was cushioned and very comfortable. There were pictures of Randy's family on the wall, and plants on the window sill facing south. A clear effort was made to make Randy's clients feel as relaxed as possible. All these efforts were to no avail. Bob felt as if he were in high school and was just sent to the principal's office. His normal take charge attitude was gone, and Randy could see that Bob's emotions were fragile.

"Bob, I was only able to clear an hour for you, but I did clear some time this afternoon. Because I don't have much time now, I will have to ask you some questions that may be hard for you to answer, but if we are to get to the bottom of this we can't waste time."

"That's fine Randy, whatever it takes."

"Tell me how this first started."

"Well, a few days ago I came home from work, and Mary had left me a note saying she was going away for a few weeks to clear her head. She said she would call to let me know she was alright, and for me not to worry."

"What was she clearing her head about?"

"Randy, I don't know," Bob said, almost in tears, "this was the first indication I had that something was wrong."

"You mean Mary never gave you any indication that something was bothering her?"

"No . . . well . . . maybe we had talked on occasion about the time I was devoting to her and the kids, but everyone goes through that. You should understand with your schedule, it isn't possible to be home every night at 5:30. I have responsibilities and meetings that are a requirement of my job. I thought she understood."

"So you feel that this is the reason she left, because you aren't home enough?"

"I have gone over this in my head time and time again, and the only other possible reason is that Mary is involved with someone else."

"Do you have any reason to believe that?"

"No proof if that is what you are asking, but why would a woman with a family take off in the middle of the day if it wasn't to be with someone else?"

"Have you ever suspected Mary of being with someone else?"

"Not before this, but Carey and I were talking one day after Mary left,"

"Carey?"

"You know Carey, my secretary?"

"Yes, I know Carey. So you talk to her about your personal life, your problems?"

"Carey is a good friend, she noticed that I was upset one day, and it all spilled out. She has been a big help. She has helped me keep my sanity over these past few days."

Randy was making notes the entire time Bob was talking, but at this moment he was sitting still, staring at Bob as if trying to separate his thoughts from the words Bob was insisting was true.

"No Randy, you are wrong, there is nothing between Carey and me. We are friends, that's all nothing more."

"Carey is a beautiful woman, and very intelligent."

"Randy, I love my wife; no one else has ever interested me. I know that Carey cares for me, probable more than a secretary should for a boss, but I have never given her any encouragement. She knows how I feel about Mary, and she knows how important my family is to me."

"So Carey thought Mary might be involved with someone else?

"I'm not sure who came up with the idea, it just made sense. Nothing else did."

"Bob, let me ask you some questions about your discussions you have had with Mary. You said you can't be home every night because of your other obligations; tell me, what are your jobs around the house."

"My jobs?"

"Tell me what your normal week is like. Bare with me Bob, I'm trying to get a handle on your daily routine."

"Well, Monday night I have bowling at 8:00, Tuesday night I have a board meeting at the bank at 7:00, but I usually go home for supper and then come back to the bank. The meetings are usually short, and I'm almost always home by 9:00. On the second Wednesday of the month I have Chamber of Commerce Board meetings, but the rest of the month I don't have a meeting. Thursdays I usually play golf after work, but I am home by 8:00 at the latest. Fridays I golf early, right after work. Saturday I usually mow the grass, repair anything that needs it, Sunday is my day to relax, watch television, or have a cook out, nothing strenuous. That pretty much is my week."

"What about family time?"

"We try to go out to eat Fridays, but with the kids schedules now days, it is hard to find the time when we are all together."

"Do you go to church on Sundays?"

"Sure, I go to church . . . well, once in awhile. Mary goes every Sunday, but I try to go every other Sunday, or every third Sunday anyway.

"And when is your time for you and Mary, just the two of you?"

"Well, we usually have most evenings together. We watch a little television, or read, or just spend time together."

"I see."

"Randy, come on, we've been married almost twenty years, Mary knows I love her."

"What makes you say that? I didn't say anything about not loving Mary?"

"You were beginning to sound a lot like Mary, during some of the discussions I told you we have had. Mary understands I do love her, or else I wouldn't be working so hard for her and the kids. She gets in these moods every now and then. When she does, I give her a little extra attention, take her out to eat and dancing, she loves to dance, and then she is fine for awhile until the next time, you know these women and their moods."

"Yes, I know their moods. Tell me Bob, what are your jobs around the house, do you cook, clean, anything like that?"

"Me? No, Mary takes care of the women's work."

"Women's work; okay . . . what about grocery shopping, paying bills, painting, getting birthday gifts . . ."

"Randy, what's going on? Mary does all these things; she has for years, what does this have to do with what is happening here?"

"Bob, it has been a few years now, but if you remember, I went through a divorce myself. Being a lawyer, I thought that I knew all the pit falls people have, and I had always thought that my marriage was about as perfect as it could be. Listening to you brings back a lot of memories. It has taken me a number of years to understand, and I also give credit to Ann for helping me grow as a man. After my marriage broke up and when I was ready to date again, I was lucky enough to meet her. When we started dating, I had a schedule almost like yours. In fact I was eager to let Ann take over the chores that Chris had done."

"Randy, what does this have to do with me?"

"Bob, one day I got home and expected dinner on the table, and nothing was there. Instead, Ann had made a list of the household chores. She was prepared, with everything written down, the things she does and the things I did. She also had written down my schedule. We spent most of the evenings that week going over our life together. What I expected and what she expected. You see, Ann had been married before too, and she knew what she wanted in a second marriage. She had worked through her problems in her mind, and had decided that no matter who she married, things were going to be different the second time around."

"I still don't understand the connection."

"I'm telling you this, because if you want to try and keep your marriage intact, and it sounds like you do, you have to first understand what it is that Mary has been trying to tell you. It isn't a woman thing, as you put it, it is a people thing. When one of your employees does a good job, what do you do?"

"I try to tell them I appreciate their effort, or I put them in for a bonus."

"What do you do for Mary, besides an occasional dinner and dancing?"

"What point are you trying to prove?" Bob was starting to get a little irritated. Randy wasn't making any sense. What did all of this have to do with Mary leaving him?

"Bob, I have listened to your weekly schedule, and it sounds almost identical to what mine was before my divorce. Our meetings are for different reasons, but my time away from home was the same. I missed the kid's things at school, I let Chris do the chores around the house, I felt when I came home, that time was my own. What I forgot was that Chris was a woman; she wasn't my maid, my housekeeper, or my nanny. She needed to know that I loved her by my actions. She had to know how special she was. I didn't take the time to notice what I was doing, and when she pointed it out to me I thought if I paid special attention to her for awhile, everything would be okay."

"And did you?"

"I did for a few days, and then I got back into my old habits. What I didn't see was that Chris worked a full day also, got home, made meals, did dishes, ran errands for the kids, and when she finally was able to sit down it was about nine or ten at night, and she still hadn't done anything for herself. I took no responsibility for the house or my family."

"But she let you do it didn't she?"

"Yes, you are right, she did, but when it finally became too much for her, I had already set my life-style and I liked it just fine. I didn't want to change, and it never occurred to me that if I didn't change, I was risking the thing that was most important to me, my family. Bob, I'm telling you this so that you can go home and think about what I have told you. It sounds so much like what I have lived, that I hope you can learn from my mistakes. If you love Mary like you said you do, I would suggest that you get some help, some counseling."

"Counseling? You've got to be kidding? I don't need counseling."

"You can say that as we are here discussing your marriage that is about to fall apart? Are you listening to yourself? Now is not the time to be proud."

"I'm sorry, but I can't go to a stranger and tell him my problems. How do I know what his life is like? He is supposed to help me with my life if he can't handle his own?"

"Bob, listen to yourself. If you can't face a councilor, then you will have to make a special effort to talk to Mary, and to understand her feelings. I suspect she doesn't feel loved, she feels more like an employee that a wife and lover, and an employee that isn't appreciated. It is up to you to make her feel like a woman again. It won't be easy, but if you care, you have to make the effort. I don't mean a temporary dinner and dancing, I mean a real change of your priorities in life, and Mary has to be the number one. Don't let her slip away Bob, there are too many people out there waiting for you to do just that, they are waiting to pick up the pieces of your marriage. I know, I couldn't believe all the men that could see in Chris the things I took for granted."

Bob sat in Randy's office not saying a word. This was his last chance, and he finally realized it. He had let everything go too far. He hadn't listened to Mary when she had talked to him. He chalked it up to being a "woman thing", and thought it would pass, but as he listened to Randy, he realized that if Mary would give him another chance, it would be his last chance, and he had to decide if he could change, and if he wanted to, he had to decide now.

"Bob, there is one more thing we need to get into before you leave. When I talked to Mary, she said you were entertaining two women while she was gone. What is that all about?"

"What?"

"That's what she said, and she was quite adamant about it. Are you involved with anyone else? I have to know the truth."

"Randy, there is no one else, for the last time. I love Mary. This is crazy, there is no one else!"

"Okay, I believe you, there must be some explanations for this. What I want you to do is go home and think about what we talked about. I will try to get a hold of Mary and set up a meeting. Now, are you sure you are ready to change your patterns? I have the feeling that Mary can't continue on as she had all these years. The change has to come from you, and not for just a few days, it has to be a permanent change."

"Randy, I'll do anything. I have to save my marriage."

"Good, I was hoping you would say that. Come back around three this afternoon, and maybe I'll have a point at which we can start."

Chapter 19

"Can I help you?" Carey paused from her work, and was looking into the most beautiful blue eyes she had seen in a long time. She mentally assessed the man standing in front of her desk. No wedding ring, the rugged, handsome, beer commercial type. He had a beautiful tan, something that was earned in the sun while working, and all this framed by beautiful blonde hair, naturally wavy.

"I would like to speak to Bob if he has a minute." Jeff noticed Carey immediately. She was beautiful and she knew how to use her assets. Her make up was flawless, her long light brown hair hung in soft waves over her shoulders. Her dress was slightly revealing, not quite appropriate for a bank, yet not obviously out of place. You could tell that she had worked at keeping her body in perfect condition, and she knew the effect that she could have on men. Jeff was a good judge of character, and a red flag immediately went up as he talked to Carey.

"Bob's not in his office today, but I can set up an appointment with you for some other time." As Carey talked she knew that Jeff was someone she would have wanted to get to know, but Bob was her priority now, and nothing was going to distract her.

"No, I'm from out of town, and I wanted to surprise him."

"Do you want to leave a message?"

"No, I still want to surprise him, can I get his address or telephone number?"

"I'm afraid he has a meeting tonight with the Chamber of Commerce, and it will be quite late before he gets home."

Jeff thought that Carey knew a lot about Bob's personal schedule for his secretary, but quickly discarded his suspicions; after all she was probably very efficient.

"Are you sure you don't want to leave a message, I might be talking to him later."

"Later meaning tonight?"

"Possibly."

So . . . Jeff thought, this was more than a secretary, she talks to him after hours too.

"No, make sure you don't say anything, I want to surprise him. I'll check back tomorrow."

Jeff had his first link to solving Mary's heartache, and no matter what it took, he was going to do this for her.

As Jeff turned to walk out of the bank, he stopped and returned to Carey's desk.

"I'm new in town, and by myself, how would you like to have supper with me. Now don't get me wrong, I'm not making a pass or anything, I'm just interested in having company for supper."

Carey looked over the stranger cautiously. He was extremely attractive, and it had been a long time since she had a night out, why not.

"I have to work until about 5:15, if you want to meet me outside the bank, I'd love to show you the town."

"Good, my name is Jeff Nelson; I'll pick you up out front at 5:15."

"No, I'll drive my own car, but you can follow me."

"Sounds good to me."

Carey watched as Jeff turned and walked out of the bank. What a great looking guy. The way he walked showed confidence in each stride. This could be a very interesting evening.

As 5:00 rolled around, Carrie put all of her work away, and made a trip to the ladies room to touch up her make up. She was a beautiful woman, but she also had learned the art of using just enough make up to create a natural look, yet enough to compliment her.

Carey returned to her desk it was 5:15. She took her purse from her desk, closed Bob's door and headed for the front door. She met a few of the tellers on her way out, and they all left the building together. As she stepped through the doorway, she saw Jeff waiting in front in a red mustang. He had the rugged good looks of an actor, and immediately drew the attention of the other tellers. Jeff saw Carey and waved, flashing his best smile her way.

"You lead the way," he yelled to her.

"Who is that?" the girls asked in unison."

"Someone I just met," Carrie answered and tossed her hair as she headed for her car. She loved being the envy of everyone else, and she could see it in everyone's eyes.

Bob was her main interest, but it will be fun to have a distraction for one evening.

Jeff followed Carey to a small bar and grill not too far from town. When they pulled into the parking lot he noticed that it was full of cars, indicating a number of people had already made it to the bar after their own office hours.

Carey got out of her car, and Jeff pulled up next to her.

"If you don't mind, this looks like it might be a busy place. Do you have a second suggestion, someplace where it might be a little quieter, and someplace where I can actually hear you talk?"

Carey smiled, "Sure, I know just the place, nothing fancy, but they have good food, and the atmosphere is quiet."

"Sounds great, hop in and I'll drive."

"No, that's alright, give me a little room and I will back up and lead the way."

As Carey got back in her car, she smiled to herself. He wants to be with her in a quieter place. He must have really been taken with her, although this was not unusual. It was unusual that she would accept an invitation from a stranger the first day she met him, but then he knew Bob, so he must be okay.

Carey pulled into Maria's and shut her engine off. Jeff was right behind her, and he flashed his terrific smile at her once again as he pulled in behind her. The girls were right, he was a looker, and she was glad to have him on her arm as she walked into the restaurant.

"I hope you like it here. They have pizza, Italian food or sandwiches if you prefer."

"It's perfect," Jeff said, as he looked around to find a room dimly lit with booths that surrounded its occupants so they were able to enjoy their own world. He would have to concentrate on his mission. Carey was extremely beautiful, but his instincts told him that Carey could not be trusted; they also told him she could probably answer a lot of his questions.

Jeff ordered a beer while Carey ordered Chardonnay. As they sat there, Jeff asked Carey how long she had known Bob, and how long she had worked for him. As Carey talked, Jeff noticed that whenever she talked of Bob, she would get a special glow in her eyes. Everything she said convinced Jeff that Carey held the key to more than some simple information. If Bob wasn't involved with Carey, it wasn't because she lacked interest. It was clear that Carey was in love with Bob, and Jeff was sure that Bob could see it also. Maybe his search was over. Perhaps his instinct was right the first time, and he could go back to Mary with answers. He was hoping that he was wrong about Mary's husband, but he was convinced now more than ever, that Bob was not the caring husband that Mary had hoped. However, he would make sure before saying anything. Mary was worth all the time he could devote to her.

Chapter 20

After Mary called Randy, her lawyer, she had to stay in her room to regain her composure, and to redo her make up. Then, with a deep breath, she turned and walked back to the café. It did help having a job and people to talk to. It helped her to forget the fact that her marriage was ending, and it was her decision that started this final chapter.

"Hon, are you okay?" Dolly asked.

"I'm fine Dolly, I had a telephone call I had to make and it upset me a bit, but I'm fine now."

"Did you call Bob? Is that what upset you?"

"No . . . Dolly, I made a decision. I called my lawyer and told him to start divorce proceedings. It's foolish for me to continue as I have. I'm not happy in my marriage. I'm not happy away from it, and now I've learned that what I thought were problems between Bob and I, now involves at least two other women, and maybe more. This is something more than I can deal with."

"Are you sure? It is awfully hard to go back after you make a decision like this. Be sure of what you want to do, don't make a hasty decision because you are frustrated."

"I know you are trying to help Dolly, but I am sure. I have struggled with this situation, and I made my decision. I feel like the weight of the world has been taken from my shoulders. Thanks to you, I realize that I can make it by myself. There is a whole world waiting for me. I can go back home, get the kids and we will start over together.

"I know you can do it Mary, but you have to know it isn't a picnic. It is just plain hard to do. There are nights that you wish you could be back in your old situation just to have another adult in the house to talk to."

"I'm sure that is true, but tell me Dolly, would you want to go back to your previous marriage?"

"Me? Heavens no! But you aren't me."

"I know, and my problems aren't the same as yours were, but don't you see, we still go through the same emotions, the same grieving over a lost relationship. Nothing can make that any easier."

"I guess you're right. We are all the same, and if we help each other, maybe we can learn from each others mistakes."

"I have decided that I will finish out the week, if that is okay, and then I have to go home. I don't want to leave you short handed, but its time I get on with my life."

"I appreciate you staying that long Hon, it helped me out. Three or four days will also give you time to think your decision over, to make sure you are doing the right thing. Maybe you can talk it over with Jeff. He has a good head on his shoulders; he can usually see the right direction to take."

"I think you're right. When Jeff comes in today I'll ask his opinion. He has been a good friend to me Dolly. I don't know what I would have done without the two of you."

"You know he is kind of sweet on you don't you?"

"Jeff? No, we're just friends."

"Hon, you may be naïve, but I have seen the way Jeff looks at you. If he weren't such an honorable person he may have done more than just look at you. You could do worse you know."

"Dolly, I think you are letting your imagination work overtime."

Just then the telephone rang, and Mary could hear Dolly's voice light up when talking.

"Well Hi Hon, we were just talking about you. She sure is, hold on a minute. Mary, guess who; your friend."

Mary took the telephone ignoring the emphasis Dolly had put on the word friend.

"Hello."

"Hi Mary; its Jeff. I thought I would give you a call. I won't be home tonight, trouble with my truck, and I have to stay over one more day."

"Oh, will I see you tomorrow?"

"Is everything okay? You sound upset?"

"I was hoping we could talk tonight. I made a big decision today and I wanted to hear your thoughts on it."

"A big decision? Now what might that be?"

"I don't want to discuss it on the phone . . . oh Jeff, I called my lawyer today and told him to file for divorce. I have been thinking about it for the last few days, and it doesn't make sense that I keep holding onto something that Bob has obviously given up long ago."

Jeff was silent, trying to process Mary's outburst. If he had to be honest, this was something he had hoped would happen. Mary was the best thing to happen to him in a long time. He had given up hoping that he would meet someone as honest and caring as she. He also realized that he was in her hometown waiting to talk some sense into her husband. Now all he wanted to do was to turn and run back to Midland as fast as he could, take Mary in his arms, and for the first time tell her how he really felt about her.

"Is that what you really want to do?" Jeff finally asked.

"I don't know, I know I can't continue on this way, and Bob has made it clear to me he doesn't want to talk to me. What other choice do I have?"

"I tell you what; we'll talk when I get back. You get some sleep, and maybe tomorrow I can help you sort through this."

"Thanks Jeff, you are a good friend."

As Jeff hung up the telephone he knew that he would try and talk to Bob tomorrow. Mary loved him, and they had children. To throw away a marriage of 20 years would hurt too many people. He was her friend, and a friend doesn't stand by and watch their friends get hurt without trying to help, even if every bone in his body is yelling at him to turn and go home. Mary had to be his first consideration now. If after trying all he could, she still wanted this divorce, then he would be there for her and hope that she would want him beside her.

Chapter 21

"Sorry to keep you waiting Carey, I had to check in with my boss. I will have to leave tomorrow morning if I am to make my schedule on time."

"You said your truck was being fixed in Milwaukee?"

"Right, I rented a car and thought that I would stop in and surprise Bob. Is he still married to that sweet thing, Mary?"

"Jeff, I wouldn't ask Bob about Mary if I were you, things are going a little rocky for them now. How well do you know Mary anyway?"

"Not well at all. I met her once and she impressed me as the perfect wife." Jeff decided to let Carey think that he didn't know her too well because she might give him more information.

"Not that perfect. A few days ago she up and left Bob and the kids without a word, and left just a note."

"You're kidding! I would never have guessed."

"You're not alone. Bob was devastated. He has all he can do to keep himself together."

"What do you think happened?"

"I'm not sure, but another man makes sense to me. Why else would Mary leave Bob and her family?"

So, that is where Bob got the idea that Mary was involved with someone else. It was planted in his mind by none other than Carey. I wonder what else she said to Bob about Mary.

Suddenly Carey reached her hand across the top of the table and covered Jeff's hand with hers.

"I think we have talked enough about Bob and his problems," Carey said seductively. She then turned Jeff's hand over and followed the creases in his hand. "You know, I do a little palmistry, would you like to know what I see in your palm."

"I don't know if I believe in that, but sure, go ahead, and give it your best shot."

Carey took one of her fingers and followed a line from the base of his finger to the edge of his palm, very slowly and sensuously. She then looked into his eyes, cocked her head to the side and smiled slightly.

"It says here that you are a kind and honest person. You will have a long life with not too many major problems. I see a tragedy early in your life, and I see you work very hard."

"You see I work very hard? I never knew you could tell that by looking at my hand."

"I cheated, I felt your calluses," Carrie giggled. "Oh and there is one last thing, it says that you kiss divinely."

"And where does it say that?"

"Here."

Carey leaned over the small table and kissed Jeff gently on the lips.

"It's my job as a palmist to make sure that my readings are correct."

"And was it?"

"I think so, but I really need to check again later just to be sure."

"I never stand in the way of science, but it is getting late, and I do have a big day tomorrow. Shall we finish this experiment outside?"

Carey looked at Jeff, and he could see that she was disappointed. He was sure she had more in mind than a good night kiss, but he was just as determined not to get involved with anyone like her.

"Maybe you're right Jeff, tomorrow is coming fast. I'm glad you suggested dinner, I really enjoyed myself."

Jeff had to think fast, he needed Carey on his side if he was to find out what was at the bottom of Bob's situation.

"I mean it when I said we should finish this outside. I am not letting you get away quite yet. I also want to be able to see you again. I come through here quite often, do you mind if I call you?"

"You can call." Carey was cooling off fast, and Jeff had to smooth things out.

Jeff put his hand out to Carey and she put her hand in his. He stood and helped her to her feet, and then pulled her close to himself and put his arm around her and led her to the parking lot. As they approached Carey's car, Jeff turned towards Carrie.

"You are a beautiful woman Carrie; someone that I should be careful of."

"Are you trying to read my characteristics now," she said teasingly?

"I guess I am trying to warn myself."

Jeff pulled Carey closer to him looking deep into her eyes, and then brought his lips to hers. She was soft, luscious, and responded to him in a way that promised more if he would only ask.

As Jeff released her and backed away, every muscle in his body was yearning for more, when his mind remembered Mary, and the hurt and pain she was going through. Mary was his priority, Mary was his friend, and Mary was his love. He opened Carey's door for her and leaned down and gently kissed her one more time, and closed the door.

Jeff turned and walked to his car. If Carey's window would have been opened she could have heard Jeff say, "This one was for you Mary."

Chapter 22

The next day Jeff was nervous as he approached the bank. How could he persuade Bob that he was throwing away the best life had to offer in turning his back on Mary? He didn't even know what he was going to say and now he was going to confront Bob. Jeff hesitated at the front door of the bank, but quickly opened it and walked to the information desk. If he thought about it too much he might end up on the highway heading toward Midland.

As he approached Carey's desk, he could see her hard at work. Her long hair cascading over her shoulders, and beneath her desk he could see the calves of her legs entwined as she worked at the computer. As he watched her work Jeff remembered the gentle caress of her touch just the night before. He could certainly see how easy it would be to become involved with her. Jeff wondered if it was that easy for Bob too.

"Jeff, good morning."

"Hi Carey; wow, you look as beautiful in the morning as you do in the evening."

"Well thank you."

Jeff could see that she was genuinely flattered by the comment, but he could also see that she was used to hearing words like theses.

"Carey, I would like to see Bob, but like I told you last night, I want to surprise him. Can you show me where his office is, and I'll just go in without you announcing me."

"This is against procedure . . . but since you are old friends, I'm sure he will want to see you."

"Does he have any appointments soon?"

"No, he has a clear calendar this morning. Go down this isle, and his office is the last door on the right."

As Jeff looked down the isle he could see through the glass partitions a man hard at work at his desk. He was good looking and just the type he hoped he wouldn't be. He was hoping for someone tall and skinny, or short and fat, someone sitting at his desk working the crossword puzzle in the paper, but this was not what he saw.

Jeff quickly opened Bob's door, and startled him as he snapped his attention to the stranger standing in front of him. Jeff glanced back at Carey's desk and saw her studying the expressions on Bob's face as Jeff walked into his office. He was going to have to do some fast work to pull this off without Carey becoming suspicious.

"Bob?"

"That's right."

"Hi, my name is Jeff," as he extended his hand to Bob, making sure to smile towards Carey. He had to make this look like they were old friends meeting again.

"Do I know you?"

"No, you don't, but I have to have a few minutes of your time. I checked with Carey, and she said you had your morning open. This really does mean a lot to me."

"So, you are a friend of Carey's?" Bob said as he sat down at his desk.

"Not exactly." How was Jeff going to explain this to Bob?

"What exactly."

"I'm a friend of Mary's."

Jeff noticed a stiffening of Bob's facial muscles. He stopped all movements as if suspended in time. All he could do was stare at the man that had just admitted to being Mary's friend.

Jeff moved so that he stood between Bob and Carey's watchful eyes. He needed some time before Carey realized that Bob was not an old friend of Jeff's.

The silence was too much for Jeff to bear, but he had no idea where to go from here.

"Bob, I know this might sound strange, but I am here to help you and Mary."

"Help? That's a strange comment to make coming from Mary's lover."

"Bob, you're wrong. I only met her a few days ago, but in that short time I have come to realize what a special person Mary is. That is why I am here, for Mary."

"Where is she?"

"I can't tell you that just yet. She is trying to sort through her life and doesn't want you to know where she is."

"So what does she want you to tell me?"

"Mary doesn't know I'm here. I'm sure she would be upset if she knew I came here on my own. Will you give me some time this morning and maybe the two of us can go have a cup of coffee and talk?"

"Quite frankly, I resent the fact that you feel you have the right to intervene. If you have only known Mary a few days, as you say, what gives you the right, or the knowledge of our marriage to even talk to me?"

"Bob, if you love Mary, why wouldn't you give me a few hours to find out if I might have something to say that might help the two of you? That is, if you love Mary."

Bob glared at Jeff when he spoke those words. Of course he loved Mary, and he resented this stranger questioning his feelings.

"Look Bob, I'm not asking for much, just an early lunch hour, enough time for us to talk, and then you can come back and continue your day like nothing interrupted it. The only thing I ask is that you not tell Carey who I am. I told her I was an old friend of the family, and I persuaded her into letting me surprise you. Just let her continue to think that we are going to catch up on old times. Two hours, what is two hours compared to someone as special as Mary?"

Those words stung as much as Jeff's earlier ones when he questioned Bob's love for Mary. He looked at Jeff's expression and could see that he truly wanted to help, but he also saw a man that was far more committed to Mary than he wanted to admit.

"Two hours. But that's all. We can go to the County Club and have coffee and then lunch. There is a private room I use for out of town customers, and no one will disturb us. I'm no ones fool Jeff. I'm interested in hearing what you have to say, but I don't trust you. I will play your little game for now, but if you don't convince me you are telling me the truth. I will leave, no matter what ploy you use, understand?"

"Understood."

With that said, Bob picked up his telephone.

"Carey, call the club and reserve the private dining room for Jeff and me. Don't make any appointments for me until after two, I might be back earlier, but I don't want to cut our visit short." After returning the telephone to its stand he examined the man standing before him. Bob was always a good judge of character, but a screen of emotions stood between his good judgment and logic. An uneasy feeling warned him not to go, but his curiosity won out. He had to find out what he knew about Mary, and more importantly what Mary meant to him.

"Okay Jeff, you have my attention for two hours." With that said he put on his suit coat and the two men walked out of the office.

As they passed Carey's desk, Jeff smiled and winked at Carrie.

"Thanks Carey, I owe you one."

Chapter 23

As Bob and Jeff entered the Country Club grounds, Jeff noticed a small but elegant sign announcing the property as private. The tennis courts were the first to greet them. If it were not for the heights of the fences, the strategically placed shrubbery would have screened it all from view. The drive wound around trees that were saved as the drive was installed, creating a gentle curving of the road with an atmosphere of peace and serenity. As they approached the club house it looked very common, not at all what Jeff had expected. The club house was a plain white building with windows looking out each side overlooking a different view of the grounds. No pillars, nothing fancy. They were greeted by two large oak doors with ornate carvings that had the look of having just been polished. As Bob opened the door and lead the way, Jeff noticed that the interior was much more formal than one would have guessed from the outside. The paintings and the carpeting was done with exquisite taste. The chandelier was small, but sparkled, radiating light from each crystal.

"Good morning Mr. Knudson", the hostess said. "We have the private dining room ready for you, is there something we can bring you now?"

"Yes, you can bring in coffee for both of us, and then later we will order lunch."

Jeff watched Bob with amazement. Here was a man of obvious importance in the community and yet was unable to understand the simplest needs of his wife, the person that should be most important in his life.

When they entered the private dining room, Jeff saw an oak conference table before him, large enough to accommodate ten people comfortable. The chairs were upholstered in beige and brown tweed, and were on large casters to move easily on the beige carpet. Next to the conference table was a smaller round table, the same kind of chairs drawn under it, and a large ash tray of heavy glass. Bob immediately walked to the round table and motioned to Jeff to join him. The door opened, and a waitress entered carrying a pitcher full of coffee, two coffee cups and containers of sugar and cream. She placed them on the table and left the room closing the door behind her. Bob poured two cups of coffee, giving one to Jeff, and then paused, looking Jeff in the eyes.

"Well you have my undivided attention now. Why don't you explain who you are and how you know Mary?"

Jeff hesitated, not knowing where to start. Why should he be trying to help Bob and Mary get back together? Bob had his chance with her, and if he continued, he may lose any chance he has with Mary.

Bob was confused by his hesitation. After all, Jeff was the one that had looked him up and insisted on this meeting.

"Alright, I'll start this conversation, where did you meet Mary and when?"

Jeff started his story of how he met Mary. It had only been a few days from their first meeting, but he felt closeness towards her that he couldn't explain. As he told Bob of Mary's job and about her living at the motel, there was an excitement in his words. Bob could hear in his voice and see it in his expressions that Jeff had fallen in love with his wife, and yet he was taking the time to try and mend whatever rip there was between them. As Bob listened to his words he tried to analyze Jeff with no results.

Suddenly Bob's attention was drawn to the words that Jeff had just said.

"You know that Mary has talked to our lawyer about a divorce?"

"Yes, but I also know that Mary loves you very much, and until she faces you and tries to work out your difficulties, I don't think she could ever be happy with anyone else."

"And that is where you come in right? You are the 'anyone else' you are talking about."

"I won't deny that I care for Mary. She is more kind and gentle than anyone I have ever met. I would do anything for her, and that includes trying to help her be happy."

"Why? It doesn't make sense, why don't you just sit back in the wings and let her file for divorce?"

Jeff sat back and sighed as if every last breath that was in him escaped.

"A long time ago I read that love is like a butterfly, you must hold it in open palms. If you were to hold too tightly, you will break its spirit or break its wings, but in any case it would die. If, while you are holding it, it flies away and doesn't come back, you will miss it, but the memories of the time it spent with you would be beautiful. If it flies away and then comes back to you, you will have found real love, and it will be with you forever . . . Mary is my butterfly, but I must give her the space to fly."

Bob saw the glisten of tears in Jeff's eyes and saw the kindness in his face. It was Just the type of person that Mary would attract. He wondered if the tables were turned would he make the effort Jeff was, and he could not answer that question.

Chapter 24

As Mary filled each coffee cup she found herself thinking of Jeff and wondering when he would be stopping by the café. She desperately wanted to talk to him, to explain her outburst on the telephone telling him of the divorce. She hadn't wanted to tell him this way, but it all came pouring out before she had a chance to stop. As each new customer came in the café she would secretly wish they would go away. All she needed now was Jeff to talk to, and Jeff to hold her hand and tell her everything would be okay.

Mary noticed that someone had come into the café and was sitting at the counter. She grabbed a coffee cup and the pot of coffee and turned toward the customer. It was Jeff, giving her his warmest smile, the one she had been waiting for all day.

"Jeff, I wondered when you would be stopping by. Is everything okay with your run?"

"Yes, I got everything worked out. I couldn't stop thinking of you the whole time."

Mary blushed a little, but was secretly pleased at Jeff's words. Dolly may be right, Jeff may have a thing for her, all Mary knew, she always felt wonderful whenever she was with him. He knew the right thing to say to make her feel like a person, someone important to him.

"Are you just about ready to quit for the day? I thought maybe we could go next door to The Office Bar and get a burger. Then maybe you can explain our conversation on the telephone."

"Let me check with Dolly, but I'm sure she will say it's alright."

Jeff wasn't sure what he was going to tell Mary about his talk with Bob. He could see that Bob really did care for Mary, but he couldn't understand how Bob could be so blind where Mary was concerned. How could he have let things get so out of control to the point that Mary felt she needed to leave before she could get his attention?

"Jeff . . . Jeff. Hey a penny for your thoughts. Dolly said I could leave if you are ready?"

"Great, let's get out of here. I'm ready for some food, how about you?"

"That sounds wonderful. Just to be able to sit and talk to you is all I need. It is amazing how I have come to depend on you in this short time."

Jeff smiled at Mary, and helped her on with her sweater. He placed his hand on her back to guide her, and as soon as he touched her he knew he was where he wanted to be. He was so comfortable with her, and he had missed that feeling while he was away.

They walked into The Office Bar. It almost seemed deserted, but neither of them noticed. Sheila came over to see what she could get them and again, had eyes only for Jeff.

"Hi Jeff, it has been awhile. Have you been out of town?"

"Yes I have Sheila. It's good to be back. How have you been?"

He could see the sparkle in her eyes as he asked about her, perhaps a hope that it was more than a casual inquiry.

"I've been fine; I just missed your smile that's all."

"Sheila, why don't you bring us two brandy/ 7's, and then we will eat a little later.

"I'll get them right away."

When Sheila left, Jeff turned to Mary. He reached out and could feel her hesitation as he took her hand in his. She had such small delicate hands, which became lost in his. As he looked into her eyes he did not want to discuss Bob or Mary's earlier conversation about asking for a divorce, but he could see in her eyes that she needed to talk about it, and he could bare the pain in his heart as long as he was able to talk to her and be close to her.

"Now, what's this about talking to your lawyer?"

Jeff, I made a decision. I have been unhappy for years. I have talked to Bob about it on many occasions, but his work and his meetings are more important to him than me or the kids. I have decided that I will file for divorce and make arrangements for the kids and me to live together. I don't care if we have the house or if we have to move somewhere else. I just need to get out of this marriage and move on with my life. I am still fairly young, and I have a lot of years left, I don't want to regret them when I'm 80."

"Did you talk this over with Bob?"

"No, I haven't been able to. He left word with his secretary that he didn't want to talk to me, and when I called home, I got that woman who answered. To be honest

I don't want to talk to him again. Whenever I do, all I get is heart ache."

"What about your children? Have you talked to them? Do you know how they feel?"

Mary's eyes immediately began to tear, fueled by the sadness in her heart.

"My kids," she said as she bowed head, "why does it always have to hurt the children? Jeff, I don't know how they feel about the two of us, but they are the reason I have never faced my own problems. I was afraid of what it would do to the kids. I've watched all the talk show programs of how a divorce can mess up a child, sometimes for life. I couldn't do that to my children. But suddenly, it was as if I couldn't face another day without dealing with my problems. I had to find an answer, and I kept coming up with the same solution. The solution I thought about years ago, but then I would always push it to the back of my mind. Finally it has come time to face it no matter how painful it might be. I have to get a divorce, for my sanity."

Jeff watched the pain in her face pleading with him to understand. Her tears gently streamed down her face not with sobs, but peacefully as if he were watching part of her soul die before his eyes.

Jeff took Mary's hands in his and covered them as if to protect her from the sadness.

"Mary, look at me." As Mary raised her eyes to Jeff, he was overwhelmed with a peace he could not understand. Her touch brought a calming effect he had not known before, and he hesitated, afraid he would break the spell by talking further.

"Do you feel it?" Jeff said. "The calm? Whenever I'm with you and I touch your hand, it is as though the rest of the world doesn't mater. I am lost in a feeling, a feeling of being complete. Even when I'm away from you, all I have to do is touch my hand, as if you are touching it, and I can bring you into my heart and my mind. I felt it before, but it is so strong now, do you feel it? Do you understand what I am saying?"

"Yes, I do, I feel it every time I'm with you. Maybe that is why I trust you so."

"It is as if we are soul mates, destined to have met. Mary, if you believe that too, I'm going to ask you to do something you may not want to do."

Mary's look at Jeff was puzzled.

"You will never know how difficult this is for me to ask you, but Mary, I want you to go back home and talk to Bob. I'm sure he will listen this time. I'm sure the last few days have given him a lot to think about. I know he loves you, how could he help but not?" Jeff stopped realizing he was too close to telling Mary how he really felt about her.

"No Jeff, I have done this too many times only to have things go back to the usual in a short time. I need someone to love me, someone that shows me and tells me, not someone that will say, you know I love you."

"All-right, do me a favor; before you completely turn your back on your marriage, do one thing. Go back home and see for yourself how Bob is. Find out if he is partying like you think, or if he is lost without you."

"Jeff, you aren't listening to me, I don't want to talk to Bob again. I have done it too many times in the past. I have to move on, I hurt too much, there has to be something else for me."

"If you don't want to talk to Bob, who else could you talk to that would know what was going on in his life; if there really is anyone else in his life. Is there anyone close to him you can trust?"

"No, Bob is a very private person, a loner. Wait, there is one person; Carey, his secretary. She is very loyal, but I think I can get her to tell me the truth about what Bob is doing. But Jeff, his other relationships are just the icing on the cake; we have not been in touch with each other for years."

"I understand that, but if you could verify this, it might make your decision easier on yourself. It might be more painful, but it will relieve the blame from your shoulders."

"I don't know Jeff, I understand what you are saying, but I don't know."

"Please Mary, for me. It will help, I'm sure of it."

Mary hesitated, and in hesitating she felt a wave of calmness fall on her as Jeff squeezed her hand. She smiled and slowly shook her head.

"OK Jeff, for you. I'll do this for you."

Chapter 25

The morning took on a new look for Mary. She awoke without the smothering sadness she had known for the last week. She knew the next few days would be difficult, but in making this decision it had freed her. She felt lighter. Each day had become easier since deciding on the divorce, and she was even able to face the customers at the café with an enjoyment of people that she had forgotten. Mary had always been a people person, but over the years Bob had harnessed that, and she now found that she had very few friends. This was one thing that Mary knew she would correct.

As she cleared away each table from the breakfast rush, she was a little sad at realizing she probably would not be back. She had made friends with the regulars, and enjoyed each person, even enjoying their differences.

Mary smiled to herself, she would miss Jeff most of all. He has been so supportive over the last few days. It was nice to go to dinner without any heavy discussions, and Jeff understood that not mentioning Bob or her marriage. She knew she was strong enough to do what had to be done for herself and her family.

"Dolly, everything is cleaned up and you should be ready for the lunch crowd in a few hours. I think it is time for me to go."

Dolly gave Mary a hug.

"Honey, you take care of yourself, and if you ever, ever need a friend to talk to, you know I'm only a phone call away."

"Thanks Dolly. I do know that. I can't tell you how much you have helped me. I don't know what I would have done without your shoulder to cry on."

"So what's next?"

"I'm driving back home. I'm all packed ready to go, and I am going to have a meeting with Bob's secretary at my house at noon."

"Bob's secretary?"

"Yes, I have to close this chapter, and I need to know a few things before I can. Carey has always been a friend, and I think she can answer a few questions before I see my lawyer."

"Jeff didn't come around for coffee this morning?"

"No, we said good-bys last night. He had an early run today so he wasn't able to stop in. I'll miss him Dolly. He is a very special man."

With that said Mary gave Dolly a last hug, and turned and walked out of the café. It was difficult to walk away, but good to be going home.

Chapter 26

As Mary approached her house heaviness surrounded her heart again. She was glad to be home, but the lightness she had felt the last few days was gone and replaced with a dreading she knew she would have to face.

Driving into her driveway she saw Carey waiting in her car by the house.

Carey saw Mary in her rear view mirror.

Ever since Mary had called her and asked her to meet her at her house during her lunch hour, she was dreading this meeting. What did she want to talk to her about? Why didn't she just get it over with and divorce Bob?

"Thanks for meeting me Carey, come on in."

Mary pressed the garage door opener and the two of them walked into the house.

As Mary opened the door, a feeling of being where she belonged overwhelmed her, and she shuttered with the realization that this was all going to end in a very short time.

"Mary, I'm not sure why you asked to see me" Carey started.

"Carey, sit down for a few minutes, please. You know that I have been gone for a while, and I'm sure you know by now that Bob and I are having some problems."

"Mary, I'm aware of some tension, but Bob doesn't confide in me."

"I thought maybe you could straighten out a few things that I am confused about. I know you are loyal to Bob. I'm not asking you to betray him, but Carey I have to know some answers and I can't proceed with my life until I have them."

"Mary, I'll try to help you if I can." Carey came next to Mary on the couch and took her hands in hers. "What can I do to help you?"

"Carey I have to know," Mary stopped, trying to push back the tears that were already streaming down her face, first, I have to know what Bob said to you, how he told you that he didn't want to take my telephone calls."

Carey had to be careful how she answered this question; she had to make sure she covered herself in case Mary got back to Bob with her answer.

"Gee Mary, let me see . . . it was the day after you left, and Bob was explaining what had happened. We talked about the fact that you may have been meeting another man, and how hurt Bob was, and that you said you would be calling back in a few days. I'm sorry Mary; I can't remember exactly what he said. Does it matter?"

"No Carey, I guess it really doesn't. Things have gone too far to turn back now."

Carey snapped her head to attention. Does this mean what she thinks it does?

"Carey, one more thing, do you know a Bonnie or a Connie?"

Carey's eyes widened. What should she say? If she acts like she does maybe it will cement Mary's decision.

"Mary, you know I'm a friend, and I don't want to get in the middle of you and Bob, but since you asked, you must know something. Yes, I do know Bonnie and Connie. They are sisters, and have been seeing Bob for quite some time now."

"They have? Have you seen them?" Mary asked in painful disbelief.

"Once I saw them as they dropped Bob off at the bank. They were beautiful. Bob kissed them both and then walked into the bank. When I asked him about them he got very upset that I had seen them, and told me that it was none of my business and what I saw didn't happen."

Mary had stopped crying now and was listening more in shock. How could she not have known?

"Since that day I haven't seen them, but Bob gets phone calls from one or the other every day. I'm sorry Mary, but you asked."

"I've heard just about all I can take", came a voice booming from down the hallway.

Bob and Jeff came walking into the family room side by side.

"Bob . . . Jeff . . . what are you doing here? What is going on?" Mary asked.

"Bob . . . I . . . Mary asked me to meet her here" Carey nervously exclaimed.

"You can drop the act Carey, I heard everything you said. How could you? I thought you were my friend, my confidant? How could you say those hurtful things about me . . . those lies?"

"Bob you don't understand. I'm the one that cares about you, about your career. I have looked out for you for years. I have always been there for you. I have put your needs before mine. I was trying to help. Help you out of a situation you were tied to."

"Get out Carey, get out and don't bother going back to the bank. I will have payroll send you a severance check. You are through. I don't ever want to see you again."

Mary watched what was happening with her mouth wide open. She was watching, but her mind couldn't quite take in all its meaning.

Jeff walked over to Mary, and took her hand.

"Mary, I have to apologize to you. When I said I was in Milwaukee having my truck repaired I was really here in your hometown getting to know Bob. I also had dinner with Carey one night, and it didn't take long to realize that Carey was the source of Bob's impression that you were meeting a man. She also made up the lies about Bonnie and Connie. Mary, there are no such people. I talked to Bob, I made him listen in on your conversation, as he was taken in by Carey as much as you."

Mary looked from Jeff to Bob still unable to process what was happening.

"Mary, remember when I said you needed to find out for yourself? What you needed to find out is that Bob really does love you. He has been miserable without you. Don't let a situation that Carey has manipulated destroy your life. You have far too much to lose to walk away without trying one more time."

Mary looked at Bob. How could she go back to the same situation she came from? No, she couldn't stand the pain anymore. Carey or no Carey, she was not what this whole situation was all about.

"Mary . . . you have a good friend in Jeff." Bob said, his chin quivering as the emotion he was feeling swelled up from his heart." It's hard for me to admit, but I wish I had his understanding. He's right. We met that day and talked, and I could see that he understood you more in a few days than I ever did in all the time we have spent together. Mary don't leave me, give me one more chance. That's all I ask. I know it won't be easy, but I will try with all my might to make things right for you. I do love you, and I always will. Please, just give me one more chance, that's all I ask."

Tear were starting to flow from Bob's eyes, running down his face. This was the first time Mary had ever witnessed his emotion concerning their marriage.

Mary's head was spinning. Everything was happening so fast. Did she hear Bob right? Was he asking for a chance to work thing out? What should she do? They have had this talk before.

"Mary", Jeff said as he took her hands in his, "You know what to do don't you?"

"No, I'm so confused. I had already made up my mind Jeff, but now I don't know."

"Mary, I know this is your life, but I also know that you have too much history with Bob, too much love for your children and your family to let it all die now, especially now that Bob is willing to do whatever it takes to make things work out between you."

Mary looked at Bob and saw the tears running down his face. She could see the love in is eyes, love she hadn't seen for quite some time.

"He's right Mary, I'll do anything. Just give me another chance. Since you have been gone I realize what you do and how much of yourself you have sacrificed over the years for our family. I have never given you enough credit; I just took it all for granted. That will never happen again. Please Mary, I want to go to counseling or do anything I have to. I know that I love you and I will do anything to save our marriage. Anything, just tell me what?"

Tears flowed down Mary's face as Bob rushed to her side and wrapped his arms around her.

"I love you Mary, please give me one more chance. Let me prove to you what is in my heart."

Mary cautiously embraced Bob and then melted in his arms. A feeling of relief flooded over Mary and over Bob. They would try one more time, and this time they both would be working together.

Suddenly the door flew open, and Candy came running in.

"Mom, Mom, where are you?" Candy rounded the corner and rushed to her mother, and then stopped, seeing the tears on both her parents' faces.

"What's happening? What's going on? You are home now aren't you? You aren't leaving again?"

Rob turned the corner behind Candy but stood back, watching Candy and his parents without saying a word. He looked at his parents and then to Jeff. Who was this guy? Was he the reason that his mother left?

Mary opened her arms to her children. "Candy, Rob, come here. I am home just where I belong. Your dad and I love you both and we are going to work very hard on keeping our family together."

Mary saw the questions in Rob eyes as he looked at Jeff.

"Rob and Candy, I want you to meet Jeff. He is a very good friend of ours. He has been very supportive of our family, and very helpful."

With that Candy and Rob threw their arms around Mary and Bob and everyone shed tears of relief, even Rob. They were secure in the knowledge that they were together again, together again, as a whole family.

Jeff slipped out of the door and left without saying good-bye. He never liked good-byes, especially this kind. He loved Mary in a way he had never loved before. It didn't make it any easier to realize that. Jeff paused for just a second and glanced back at Bob and Mary with their family. They didn't see the tear as it rolled down his cheek, and they never knew that the pain in his heart was comforted by the fact that Mary was home now, home where she belonged.

Printed in the United States
By Bookmasters